DISCERNMENT AND INNER KNOWING
making decisions for the best

Joycelin Dawes

Published in 2017 by FeedARead.com Publishing

First Edition

A CIP catalogue record for this title is available from the British Library.

Enquiries: < discernmentandinnerknowing@gmail.com >
www.woodbrooke.org.uk

TABLE OF CONTENTS

Preface

This book grew out of preliminary research for an Eva Koch Scholarship in 2016. I wish to thank Woodbrooke Quaker Study Centre[1] for awarding me the scholarship which gave me the opportunity to reflect on discernment and develop some ideas. My thanks also to: fellow Eva Koch scholars – Rhiannon Grant, Anne de Gruchy and Jane Pearn for their company; my tutor, Gill Pennington, and the Woodbrooke tutor team, especially Martin Layton and Simon Best.

I am indebted to those whose insight and experience I draw on. I have gained much from the work of Otto Scharmer, Joseph Jaworski, and their Theory U colleagues. I learn continuously from the deep wisdom and richness of the Quaker tradition, particularly its liberal wing in the UK and USA. My research for the Eva Koch scholarship was a literature review of sources drawn from a bibliography for participants on discernment courses at Woodbrooke, and I quote many of these authors. My observations about discernment were further illustrated by the insights of a few people with whom I had conversations whilst I carried out research for my Eva Koch scholarship: thank you to Sandra Berry, Peter Eccles, Michael Hutchinson, Judith Moran, Danielle Walker Palmour and Jonathan Woolley. I learned more of Ignatian discernment from a conversation with Sister Una Coogan I.B.V.M. I am also deeply grateful to Nancy Bieber and Elizabeth Liebert, authors of two of my main literature sources, who responded to me with great warmth and encouragement. I also thank my critical readers, Linda Craig, Jane Reed and Deborah Rowlands for commenting on an early draft of this manuscript. It is enormously helpful for a writer to have such constructive response during the process of creation.

Finally, I appreciate the support, and, even more, the forbearance, of family and friends, whilst I spent long hours reading books and writing at the computer and, thus, made myself less available to them.

I write as a Quaker – therefore, I usually refer to Quakers as *we*, *us* or *Quakers* rather than *them*. Sometimes this is awkward so occasionally I adapt my rule to aid the flow of my writing. My readers

---

[1] www.woodbrooke.org.uk

are generally *you* as I imagine this as a conversation between you and me. Throughout I most frequently use the word *Source* rather than God, Spirit, Inward Light or similar terms. I borrow both *Source* and *inner knowing* from Theory U (explained later), intending them as impartial between those of us for whom *God* is a word that describes the mystery at the heart of spiritual experience and those of us for whom other words or none more faithfully reflect our experience of this mystery. My own sense is of a unified wholeness that is present through all creation. It is in its nature that it cannot be described but it can be recognised, and to that extent known, through the manifold ways in which it is expressed and present in our world. The path of spirituality is exploring and testing how we find this expressed in and through life. We each discern our response to what we experience as true to this sense of God (as a word to denote what I have described above) and what is not. Our purpose is then to learn to recognise the promptings and leadings that uphold and nurture its unfoldment and further expression. When I use the word *Source* I refer specifically to how Theory U addresses this kind of non-rational dimension; I often use *source* to refer to our own inner connection or relationship with this reality. *Inner knowing* may be thought of as a stream of wisdom, will-to-good, love and truth, that arises from this connection and guides us in expressing it in action and behaviour.

You, my readers, I assume to be mainly Quakers or people familiar with the Quaker way. Since I hope there may be amongst you those less familiar with Quaker discernment, worship and business methods, I explain more background and terminology than needed for a solely Quaker audience.

Lastly, I have tried to attribute quotes and material, which are referenced in the Bibliography. Where any of this is mistaken, I apologise and will willingly amend the text at the first opportunity. I have tried to interpret fairly and accurately the work of all the creators of work I refer to. Nevertheless all interpretations from my research are my own and should not be taken to reflect the views of those from whom I quote.

Chapter 1: Getting Started

"The outer work can never be small if the inner work is great.
And the outer work can never be great if the inner work is small"

Meister Eckhart

Introduction

Discernment is living in accordance with our inner knowing, a stream of wisdom and will-to-good that arises as we are in touch with our deepest inner place or source. As Meister Eckhart, the great mystic of medieval times, observed, there is an intimate relationship between the depth of this inner work and the quality of work it fosters in the world.

This enquiry explores spiritual and secular discernment through Quaker practice and Theory U. Quakers are a faith community with roots in the seventeenth century and widely recognised for putting faith into action through a spirit-led process of making decisions. Theory U is a contemporary framework for change that draws on presencing – connecting to Source and inner knowing that allows individuals and groups to shift the inner place from which they function and thus make decisions that embody a future possibility they sense might emerge.

As I found my spiritual home amongst Quakers more than twenty years ago, it seemed to me that drawing on inner knowing is a fundamental Quaker practice, both individually and in community (or corporate discernment). A favourite saying of Quakers in Britain is "Take heed, dear Friends, to the promptings of love and truth in your hearts". This seems clear advice. The paragraph continues "Trust them as the leadings of God whose Light shows us our darkness and brings us to new life" (QFP, 2016, para. 1.02). This second sentence is more problematic. Today we live in a society where we are less comfortable with experience and belief in God. What is this God who prompts feelings of love and truth in our hearts? Are such promptings the same for those who believe in God and those who are, at most, uncertain? Do we have to do anything in particular to recognise promptings in our heart? Can we distinguish between authentic and false promptings (which nevertheless seem quite loving and truthful) – which are which? What is God's Light like, and how do we recognise it? And what exactly does one do to open to the Light? And might such promptings be akin to inner knowing?

The purpose of my enquiry

I belive that exploring what discernment is and how it is practised is essential if we are to use it effectively and with integrity. The understanding and language of discernment passed down from early Friends (Quakers) – such as following the will of God – perplexes numerous established Friends and many new to Quakers alike. In a talk given to Meeting of Friends in Wales in October 2014, Gerald Hewitson remarked: "I sometimes wish that we Quakers could speak with a language for the twenty-first century – a language which speaks with the power and authority of authenticity, and which could command respect among those as yet uncalled into faith (for there is still a great people to be gathered)" (Hewitson, 2014). I am confident that Quaker discernment, built on three hundred and fifty years of experience, has a story to share with all who make decisions in the light of inner knowing. However, to share the fruits of that experience we must first understand it more clearly for ourselves. Theory U uses different language and concepts to Quakers. Yet I find sufficient resonance between Theory U and Quaker discernment to use Theory U as a way of exploring Quaker practice from the outside. Theory U is so called because it employs the letter U as a visual image, or map, of the flow of a discernment process.

Thus, the aim of my present enquiry is to survey, clarify and strengthen Quaker understanding of discernment, and test a map to support Quakers in sharing our experience of discernment within and beyond Quaker circles. By the time I complete this enquiry I hope to adapt the map I use from Theory U into a map of Quaker discernment that incorporates insights and strengths I draw from my exploration.

Why I chose to explore discernment

My understanding of discernment draws on: a personal practice of reflection and attempting to discern, for instance, promptings of love and truth in my heart; participation in local and national Quaker gatherings where decisions are discerned corporately using Quaker business method; and many years' experience of groups and organisations that, in various ways, discern decisions collectively. As a charity trustee, I know non-Quaker organisations where decisions are made in a manner similar to Quaker organisations, but where it is not perceived as discernment. Is there any substantive difference between such decision-making and Quaker discernment? The sceptic in me wonders how often Quakers talk about discernment because 'it's something special we know Quakers do' but with less clarity about what it is. My interest in discernment crystallised during six years as a trustee of Quaker Social Action (QSA), a Quaker-led organisation[2] during which I was clerk to the trustees and chair of the trustee board for five years. At the time of writing I am a trustee of Friends Provident Foundation[3] – Quaker founded but not a Quaker-led foundation – having begun as its chair of trustees for three years. Such organisations encapsulate the gifts and challenges of practising discernment whilst measuring up to the requirements of running a small business and delivering benefit to the public.

I felt prompted to explore discernment further. Each year Woodbrooke Quaker Study Centre awards a small number of Eva Koch scholarships for a limited piece of research on a topic relevant to Quakers. My proposal for a 2016 scholarship was to explore Quaker discernment by a selected review of literature used on discernment courses at Woodbrooke. Alongside this I wanted to adopt a standpoint outside a Quaker frame of reference to look at Quaker discernment afresh. I settled on Theory U as a secular framework whereby a course of action emerges from connection to Source or your deepest inner place, and paying attention to inner knowing. You might liken my enquiry to people feeling different parts of the same elephant, each describing it as they find it. My elephant is Quaker inside and Theory U outside!

My approach is to seek to understand enough of Theory U to use it as a means of exploring Quaker discernment. I search for common ground and complementarity between Theory U and Quaker discernment, as well as noting their differences. Not surprisingly, I found my enquiry raised broader questions than I had envisaged. I came to see Quaker experience of discernment as a gift to share in the

---

[2] Quaker Social Action www.quakersocialaction.org.uk/
[3] Friends Provident Charitable Foundation
   www.friendsprovidentfoundation.org/

troubled times in which we live. This is conveyed by Liz Sweeney in her article *Moving into a Deeper Communion*:

"We live in a time of profound change and upheaval, a time when social systems, culture, and human consciousness must transform if we are to meet the critical challenges we are facing. The evening news tells the story: the destruction of the earth, war, violence and hatred, materialism that ignores the needs of the poorest among us, hunger, and joblessness — miseries that come at us from every direction. Today's problems, as Einstein reminds us, 'cannot be solved with the same level of consciousness that created them'. I believe this means we need to evolve communally at the level of consciousness. It is an invitation to learn to transform the way we are together, to evolve the way we think, feel, and love when we are in relationship communally" (Sweeney, 2014).

A practical approach to discernment

Stating that discernment is living in accordance with our inner knowing does not, as it stands, tell me how to apply this concept. I need a practical litmus test that helps me make sense of discernment in my personal life and in collective decision making.

Early in my research I found a practical approach that characterises the nature of discernment as *making a decision for the best*. This emerged from a workshop led by Michael Hutchinson for Quakers in South East Scotland on concern[4], individual and corporate discernment (Hutchinson, 2016). I adopt this approach as it allows me to explore discernment from a broad point of view in language that neither prescribes nor excludes God, Spirit, Source, spirit-led, Something More, sensing the emerging future, highest future potential or other images that might specify inner knowing. I interpret 'for the best' to mean a decision or choice that is not based on self-centred preferences, bias or prejudice, nor favour narrow sectional interests. But I want to go further and qualify 'for the best' as the best *for the whole*.

---

[4] When Quakers feel pushed collectively by the spirit to a course of action (see Jane Pearn, 2017)

Thus, I explore discernment as a process of seeking, in any given set of circumstances, a decision for the best in the interests of the whole. I refer to this as making decisions for the best.

My enquiry focuses on making such decisions by opening ourselves to source and inner knowing. This might be expressed, for instance, as seeking and following the will of God; being spirit-led; seeking God's preferred future; choosing to uphold that of God; acting congruently with the values of a higher level of consciousness; creative inspiration arising from our own deeper lives; attuning to your soul, spirit or angel or that of a group or organisation, paying attention to non-rational modalities of knowing, and numerous other ways of understanding such experience.

I use the term *spirit-led* where discernment draws on what Douglas Steere, an American Quaker, calls "a life of the spirit" (Steere D. 1971, p. 7). Quaker discernment is my principal example of spirit-led discernment with some reference to Ignatian discernment[5]. I see Theory U as secular discernment, thus employing a secular language where inner knowing is likened to sensing the emerging future and bringing forth the highest future potential.

What are we doing when we discern?

From my literature review, I notice three complementary ways in which discernment is discussed. Firstly, discernment is *an activity of 'being discerning'* thus living in accordance with making choices for the best; when I refer to discernment this is the mode of discernment I most frequently mean. Secondly, discernment is *a method of collective decision-making*; it is generally clear when I am discussing this mode of discernment and later I focus specifically on communal and corporate Quaker discernment. Thirdly, writers use discernment to indicate *a precise stage in decision-making* – testing the validity of inner knowing which is recorded as a decision and validated through action; I reflect on this in later chapters.

---

[5] I sometimes refer collectively to Loring, Bieber and Liebert – three of the main sources from my literature review – as Quaker writers or writers about Quaker discernment. They are not all Quaker writers nor are they writing only about Quaker discernment but I use it in place of a longer explanation.

This tells me of three contexts when discernment is happening but not what we are doing when we discern. Margaret Benefiel, an American Quaker and director of Shalem Institute, Washington DC, describes discernment as "a process of going deeper. It is drawing on one's whole self, heart, mind, soul, and spirit … Through being deeply spiritually grounded the discerner cuts through the usual distractions and attachments that obscure accurate perception, and seeks to see reality clearly". So discernment seems to have two principal elements: a *w*holistic engagement of my self, and a process by which I can set aside the stories I'm usually telling my self about 'life' so my responses are less weighed down by the knots of my ego.

Benefiel sees discernment used in three linked contexts. When practised by an individual she calls it *individual discernment*. However, she argues, individual discernment needs "the support of a community, nurturing and grounding the person's spiritual life"; this, she says, is found in the checks and balances of accountability through *individual discernment in community*. Her third mode is in a group, organisation or community where depth and authenticity require individuals to come prepared in mind and heart for *corporate or collective discernment* (Benefiel, 2005, pp. 51-52). I embrace this three-fold model lightly as I consider discernment.

Sensing the emerging future

Discernment can be used for day-to-day matters and major issues, and by individuals, groups and organisations (who I refer to as the discerner). Typically the discerner faces a challenge, has a nagging question or issue to be addressed. All too often our response to a challenge or question is to react as we have done in the past. Sometimes we may find flexible and creative ways to respond, whether just edging forward or making a leap into the unknown to do something that has never been tried before.

We – individual, groups and organisations – may become limited if we habitually base decisions on bias or prejudice, rigid patterns of thought or narrow sectional interests. We remain stuck when we do not recognise our inability to move out of familiar patterns or resist doing so. These patterns are often unrecognised thus they are difficult to address.

Decisions for the best reach instead toward what Theory U interchangeably calls 'sensing the emerging future' and 'highest future potential'. More prosaically, this might be asking 'what can happen here?' or 'what is possible?' The idea is that by tuning in to the emerging future we can discern or touch into future potential, something that can be done, some action or way forward. This crystallises an element of what might be – the future – into a present action and facilitates experimenting with how it might work and develop. It may be a very small step or it may be radical change. The Quaker phrase 'being spirit-led' reminds us that Quaker discernment sees the emergence of this potential from a reality early Friends knew as God.

Why Theory U?

Some years ago I read a book called *Presence* (Senge, 2005). It seemed to me that the co-authors – Peter Senge, Otto Scharmer, Joseph Jaworski and Betty Sue Flowers – encountered something I imagined as akin to the experience of early Quakers. They, too, experienced how a group meeting and working together, sharing and engaging intently with each other's experience and ways of seeing, begins to think together – corporately; their insights and decisions arise from a shared inner experience where each person experiences themselves as part of a larger whole.

Presence, the authors explain, is a combination of being present and sensing; I think of sensing as having all our antennae vibrantly alive to our inner and outer environment. I was drawn by the idea of 'sensing'; this suggests an experiential approach using more than just my rational mind to reflect; it is both ruminative and deliberative. It felt congruent with Quaker experience and explained something about it in a different way. The idea that we may be able to sense, or touch into, the future resonates with my understanding that each moment is imbued with potential. We can open ourselves to working with the grain of this potential, or ignore or stifle it; but we have a choice to make and discernment implies a considered choice.

Around the same time, two of the authors, Scharmer and Jaworski, were interviewing people who seemed to have a capacity to work creatively at the leading edge in their field. They were asking them: "How is 'the new' born, how does it emerge?" Jaworski realised there was a critical moment when organisations faced an existential challenge: "the opening I saw – to develop a process whereby teams could sense the way the future wants to unfold, and to enable that unfolding. I felt that teams could guide this process by their intention, their way of being, and their choices" (Jaworski, 2012, p.234/3302 Kindle).

Whilst following up this insight, Jaworski came across the work of Brian Arthur, an economist and complexity theorist. On the basis of what he read, he and Scharmer went to interview Arthur.

In a remarkable interview, Arthur explained that connecting with our deepest inner self entails three major movements. The first thing you do, he said is observe. This kind of intense observation "might take days, or hours, or fractions of a second as in martial arts or sports"; then you "reflect and retreat – allow the inner knowing to emerge". Finally, he said, you "act swiftly, with a natural flow". Arthur continued: "This inner knowing comes from here, [pointing to his heart]. In a sense, there is no decision making," he said. "What you do just becomes obvious. A totally different set of rules applies. You hang back. You're more like a surfer or a really good racecar driver. You don't act out of deduction, you act out of an inner feeling; you're not even thinking." Arthur concluded by noting: "This approach to decision making requires time, patience, and another key ingredient: courage. It takes courage to listen to your inner wisdom. But once you hear that wisdom, making a decision becomes fairly easy" (Arthur, W Brian, 1999, pp. 9-12).

Jaworski and Scharmer mapped the three movements Arthur described onto a letter U. This became their first version of tracking the emergence of inner knowing as a U-shaped flow. From their point of view, this U diagram gave them "a preliminary understanding of the core process ... by which transformational breakthroughs in any field occur, the creation of knowledge that changes the world as we know it" (Jaworski, 2012, pp. 339/3302, Kindle).

As I explored Theory U further on a Soul of Leadership course at Woodbrooke, I found the U map spoke to me intuitively about Quaker discernment. I was attracted by applying Theory U as a map to explore Quaker discernment. Could it illuminate this perplexing, much-used but often less well-understood practice?

How my enquiry unfolds

In this chapter, *Getting Started*, I explain my enquiry and set out my working approach to discernment. This approach is intended to have a practical bent – one you might see yourself using – so I end this chapter with a reflective exercise on your own experience of discernment – making a decision for the best – to assist you as you read further. In Chapter Two I describe Theory U to the extent needed to apply it in exploring Quaker discernment. In Chapter Three, I compile an account of Quaker discernment from a limited literature review – the basis of my Eva Koch research. Thereafter I use Theory U to reflect further on Quaker discernment. In Chapter Four I explore listening as a means to opening mind, heart and will, practices central in both Theory U and Quaker discernment. Chapter Five discusses Quaker discernment in community. Chapter Six focuses on the midpoint of the U map which in Theory U is the heart of connecting with Source and inner knowing; here I consider ways we might think about this in the context of Quaker discernment and the inner place from which we make decisions for the best. The next two chapters are concerned with how Quaker discernment is confirmed and tested (Chapter Seven) and acted on (Chapter Eight). In Chapter Nine I review my enquiry and draw my conclusions. I include Reflections at the end of each chapter, a place for musing and questioning my text in some way.

I intend this text to be a practical guide. I encourage you initially to read the chapters sequentially. I use Theory U as a map and, as with any map, it is important to first grasp the map as a whole before finding your place on it and devising your own route.

Reflecting on your experience

Before going further I recommend you reflect on the questions below to bring your own experience to mind before reading about Theory U and Quaker discernment.

Recall a discerned or well-grounded decision you have made and draw on it in responding to these questions:

1. What does discernment mean to you?
2. What practices help you develop skilful discernment?

---

3. How do you experience the inner knowing at the heart of your discernment?

4. How do you 'communicate' with this source?

5. How do you discern its 'voice'?

6. How do you test and act on this?

Chapter 2: About Theory U

As my enquiry applies Theory U as a map to Quaker discernment I start by explaining something of it. Theory U is a large and complex body of material, used increasingly widely and attracting large numbers of people to online seminars. A number of Quakers have found that it seems to resonate with Quaker processes. I introduce only the essentials needed for my enquiry.

In the first place, visualise a capital letter U, with the addition of a dot at the bottom of the U (diagram 1). This indicates the key element on the U map, a point of connection with our deepest source and inner knowing. The journey down the U, then across the bottom, before travelling up the other side of the U maps Arthur's three movements outlined in the previous chapter and discussed below.

Going down

Diagram 1: Movement 1 – going down

Arthur originally described the first movement, shown as going down the U, as 'observe, observe, observe'. I prefer to think of it as 'noticing'; it is embraced in the Quaker phrase "centring down". Although not meaning exactly the same as 'noticing', this Quaker phrase directs attention away from other matters toward discernment and inward reflection. A U process moves from an initial download of ideas, assumptions and agendas to opening toward a more diverse field of knowing and understanding. Opening happens as we notice the inner movements in our mind, heart and body and consciously commit to disengaging from habitual thinking, feeling and doing – or in a Quaker phrase "coming with heart and mind prepared". Opening the mind might be perceived by Quakers as commitment to truth; opening the heart as commitment to love; and opening the will as the impulse to discern for the best. Arthur identified a difference between the cognitive, rational thinking that commonly surfaces at the beginning of a U process, and the knowing that is facilitated by the process itself. He observed: "You wait and wait and let your experience well up ... What to do becomes obvious ... much of it depends on where you're coming from and who you are as a person

... I am basically saying that what counts is where you're coming from inside yourself" (2009, p. 705/9228 Kindle).

Across the bottom of the U

Diagram 2:
Movement 2 –
going across

Arthur describes this phase as retreat and reflect, moving the discerner into a place of stillness where inner knowing emerges. Senge and his co-authors called this deep inner state presencing. In *Presence*, the authors discuss this point as "the mystery at the bottom of the U ... pre-sensing and bringing into presence – and into the present – your highest future potential. It is not just the future in some abstract sense but my own future potential as a human being." Amongst Quakers this is akin to letting in and waiting in the Light, listening for the movement of Spirit that guides discernment. Senge and his co-authors began to perceive it as "a level of reality that's not exterior to or separate from our highest self ... The important point is in exploring this future potential you aren't exploring a future someone else has written for you. It's more intimately connected with your evolving, authentic Self – who you really are. It's much more fluid, more open, more in dialogue with you ... it's being an instrument of life itself, to accomplish, in a sense what life or God, or however you want to put it, wishes for me to accomplish" (Senge, 2005, pp. 219-221).

Going up

Diagram 3: Movement 3 –
going up

Arthur epitomised his third movement as: "Act in an instant. Explore the future by doing." A decision or direction has been discerned and the movement up the U is a process of working out how to embed it in action, continuing to monitor, test and check the validity of the discernment until developed to its full potential. This is echoed in a much-quoted phrase: "Until one is committed there is hesitancy, the chance to draw back, always ineffectiveness. Concerning all acts of initiation (and creation) ... the moment one definitely commits, then providence comes too. All sorts of things occur to help one that would never otherwise have occurred" (Murray, 1951). This completes a single discernment cycle.

Diagram 4: a simple Theory U map

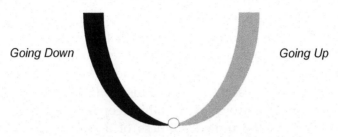

Going Down   *Going Up*

Across the Bottom of the U
Presencing: presence + sensing. Getting in
touch with a deep inner place and listening to
the inner knowing arising from within

The importance of thresholds and inner knowing

It seems to me that the transition from Arthur's first movement into the second – where the left-hand side of the U curves into the bottom of the U – marks a stage where there is often a struggle to enter this deeper stillness. Rowan Williams, past Archbishop of Canterbury, once said of his daily period of prayer that he spent most of the time trying to reach the place within him where he was able to pray and, over the course of an hour, achieved only a few minutes in a prayer of communion with God. This suggests it is not simply a smooth, one-way progression down the curve to a profound connection with the source. It is a transition that crosses a threshold.

Thresholds are significant as they mark a passage or transition "which hold[s] the possibility of moving into something new, or an opportunity for seeing with new eyes, openings to potential and transformation" (Dawes, et al., 2005, p. 12). In biblical terms this particular threshold represents passing through the eye of a needle. The phrase "eye of the needle" refers to a gate in ancient Jerusalem, where, according to the Bible, "it is easier for a camel to go through the eye of a needle than for a rich man to enter the kingdom of God". For a man to fit his camel through Jerusalem's gate in biblical times, he had to remove all the bags from the camel's back. To go through the eye of the needle at the bottom of the U, you have to offload all the baggage, thoughts, assumptions and ideas that no longer serve you, in order to gain access to 'Jerusalem' – connection with source and inner knowing.

This connection requires both a capacity to find and rest in a deep inner place and, in that stillness, an ability to listen to what the Bible calls "the still, small voice". When Elijah fled into the wilderness in fear for his life, God showed him that discerning the will of God was not always conveyed by earthquakes and fire – dramatic events and revelations – but by as little as a whisper (Kings 19:12). In Quaker discernment when a group reaches this deep inner state it is spoken of as 'gathered': "In the united stillness of a truly 'gathered' meeting there is a power known only by experience, and mysterious even when most familiar" (QFP, 2016, para. 2.39). It is equally pertinent but used less often to describe the experience of being gathered in personal practice, too. Yet cultivating and resting in personal stillness is a prerequisite for settling into a deep place in a corporate setting.

I notice a similar threshold moving from movement 2 into movement 3, a transition where the curve at the right hand base of the U begins the movement up. It is a thin place where clarity is sought in articulating to oneself or with a group the insight or inner knowing arising from listening and paying attention to the insight, intuition, wisdom or voice of God. Quaker corporate practice allows time for further exploration before the threshold into unity and action is crossed.

Our blind spot

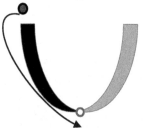

Diagram 5: The blind spot in leadership: *how* to get from downloading to presencing and inner knowing

Arthur told Jaworski and Scharmer: "Every profound innovation is based on an inward-bound journey, on going to a deeper place where knowing comes to the surface" (Senge, 2005, p. 13). Jaworski and Scharmer first thought this deeper place is accessed by being aware, conscious and sensing in the moment – presence. Then they began to understand presence itself as deep listening, of being open beyond one's preconceptions and usual ways of making sense, going to a deeper place to make choices that serve the evolution of life.

Nevertheless, Scharmer noticed a barrier between knowing about the experience of inner knowing and having a means to access it. People frequently remained locked in familiar and habitual patterns and thoughts, which Scharmer termed 'downloading'. They were unaware of their familiar habits of thinking, bias and taken-for-granted assumptions, unable to access their inner knowing whilst they remained stuck in this groove. He called this a blind spot: "this [U process] pulls us into an emerging possibility and allows us to operate from that altered state rather than simply reflecting on and reacting to past experiences. But in order to do that, we have to become aware of a profound blind spot... the place within or around us where our attention and intention originate." (Scharmer O. 2009, p. 333/9228,Kindle)

Energy follows attention: the importance of opening

In other words, Scharmer realised that energy follows attention. If our attention is locked up in existing habits of thought and reacting to the past then that is where our energy remains – it is stuck. If we want to reach a deeper place and act from inner knowing we need to switch out of this pattern in order to pay attention to opening to the stillness in which inner knowing arises. He realised the critical nature of "connecting with a deeper place from which I can operate. The key in going down the U lay in opening the mind, opening the heart and opening the will" (Scharmer, 2009, pp. 344-744/9228, Kindle).

Gradually, Arthur's simple map of three movements developed into a process where going down the U involved successively opening the mind by finding new ways of seeing, opening the heart by responding empathically to a wider field of experience, and opening the will to set aside one's own ideas of how to act in order to be present to inner knowing. It was balanced by parallel movements going up that embodied acting from and for the whole – mind, heart and will.

Opening requires suspending, redirecting and letting go

But Scharmer still didn't know *how* we could become open and navigate our way to that deep inner place where we can access inner knowing. If you are stuck in downloading the same old ways and ideas, how can you come to see with fresh eyes, walk a mile in another's shoes and be willing to follow where this leads? Scharmer's answer to this puzzle came from meeting cognitive scientist Francisco Varela who suggested a dynamic shift is needed for each kind of opening.

Diagram 6: Shifts between modes of Opening

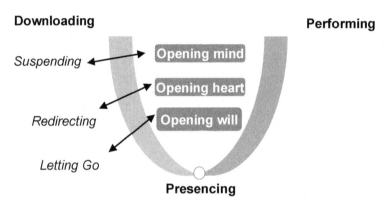

- Opening the mind is facilitated by *suspending* – slowing down, tolerating unsettling questions and possibilities rather than shutting them down, setting aside existing agendas to collect and open to other information

- Opening the heart is facilitated by *redirecting* – consciously turning attention away from preoccupation with our own thoughts, listening and learning deeply from others' experience and points of view

- Opening the will is facilitated by *letting go* – the capacity to surrender preconceived ideas in order to allow space – letting in – for new possibilities. It is likened to going through the eye of a needle as it demands willingness to be free of baggage and constraints in order to listen to the knowing that arises through presence. Passing through the eye of the needle is stepping into the unknown, and letting go of the old ways of seeing whilst opening to the intelligence of the body through the will.

Across the bottom of the U and going up

Going down prepares the way for moving into and across the bottom of the U. The still point at the bottom of the U represents the culmination of the movement down; I explore this in more detail later. Going up the right-hand side of the U is equally important. Beyond presencing, inner knowing has to be crystallised, checked, validated and acted upon: How does the new come into being? How is it made manifest? The Theory U map is completed by gateways that put inner knowing into action. We have to sustain the openness of mind, heart and will that embodies acting for the best, not only for the whole but from the whole of ourselves too.

Diagram 7: A Theory U map of a discernment cycle

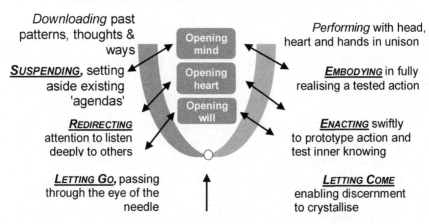

Downloading past patterns, thoughts & ways

Opening mind

Performing with head, heart and hands in unison

SUSPENDING, setting aside existing 'agendas'

Opening heart

EMBODYING in fully realising a tested action

REDIRECTING attention to listen deeply to others

Opening will

ENACTING swiftly to prototype action and test inner knowing

LETTING GO, passing through the eye of the needle

LETTING COME enabling discernment to crystallise

Presencing – connecting to source and inner knowing

- Sustaining an open mind by *letting come* – listening to inner knowing and allowing it to form and crystallise

- Sustaining an open heart by *enacting* – acting swiftly and testing inner knowing by designing a prototype to trial a decision in action

- Sustaining an open will by *embodying* – taking the tested action or behaviour (amended as needed) and bringing it to full realisation in the world.

Reflections: an overview of Theory U

- I am surprised by the interpretation applied to downloading in Theory U. Whilst an initial response to a question will contain existing opinions and judgements, it is likely to contain much useful material and information, too. I find it useful to perceive downloading as gathering all current 'data' relating to the question, remembering that includes valuable information and experience as well as attachment, fear and other negative aspects which need to be recognised and addressed. For instance, this chapter outlining Theory U and the next chapter, compiling an account of Quaker discernment, 'download' both valuable information about these two models of discernment and at the same time include taken-for-granted assumptions and inbuilt blindness to their limitations.

- The stages of going down the U and transitions from one stage to the next are, necessarily, described in a linear manner but experience is unlikely to move sequentially through the stages as depicted. It is almost certain to be more messy.

- Some commentators observe parallels between going down the U and other ways of perceiving movement and growth. For instance, seeing with fresh eyes, sensing from the field and moving into presence has been likened respectively to developing IQ, EQ (emotional intelligence) and SQ (spiritual intelligence). Whilst these intelligences are contentious in terms of establishing their scientific credence, they have gained traction as they seem to equate to ways in which we know ourselves.

- Discernment and Theory U have been discussed so far without distinguishing necessarily between discernment by an individual and collective discernment in groups and organisations. The core of the practice of discernment is the same in each case but groups and organisations often have a more clearly defined method of using discernment to make decisions. Serving as a trustee on boards of charities, both those that are not faith-based organisations and those that are spirit-led, I have observed a similarity of approach albeit with different emphasis given to the particular step of making a decision when they are spirit-led. There are similar cultures based on inclusion, respect, trust, and reference to a source of authority from which the board draws its decision; the difference is between boards that see their decision drawing on the values, wisdom and heritage of the organisation and Quaker practice of being spirit-led. But there is a grey area between what is – and what is not – discernment.

- Theory U was born in a very different milieu to spirit-led discernment. It comes from a secular setting informed by new knowledge in science, in management and large-scale transformational change, in psychology, in the psycho-dynamics of group work, and the movement of spirit in contemporary society. As Senge has observed: "The phenomenon of presencing is diverse: it is experienced and described differently by different people in different communities." Therefore, I think it likely that the different lingua franca of Theory U offers fresh possibilities for enriching conversations about different kinds of discernment for the best.

- In her article *Moving Into Deeper Communion* (Sweeney, 2014), Liz Sweeney bases her analysis of the power of dialogue on Theory U. She points out the value of developing skilful discernment: "The key to addressing the multiple unfolding crises of our time – and the future course of human development – lies in learning how to access the source (the invisible, subtle, underlying dimension) of mastery (creativity) collectively." Similarly, one of the core principles of the Center for Action and Contemplation, founded by Father Richard Rohr, quotes Gerald May: "Contemplation happens to everyone. It happens in moments when we are open, undefended, and immediately present." The principles also maintain that: "We do not think ourselves into a new way of living, but we live ourselves into a new way of thinking," and that in the words of the Dalai Lama: "Every change of mind is first of all a change of heart" (Center for Action and Contemplation).

- Opening, whether of heart, mind or will, is a progressive and iterative cycle; there is no one-stop shop! Opening is a term I take to denote processes by which we can disengage from the hotch-potch of ideas, assumptions, thoughts, biases, prejudices, experiences, accumulated knowledge etc. that populate the stream of chatter, emotion and activity that colour so much of our waking hours.

- The three modes of opening – suspending, redirecting and letting go – act as gateways for progressively opening to deeper stillness. Letting go asks the discerner to trust, to let go of everything that may be an impediment and encounter a state of profound unknowing in order to reach stillness. In Theory U, as in Christian – including Quaker – spirituality, an encounter with unknowing is at the heart of the mystery whether identified as God or the source. In Theory U, Scharmer writes: "Presencing requires us to let go of the old and open ourselves completely to something that we can sense but that we cannot fully know before we see it emerging. This moment can feel like jumping across an abyss. At the moment we leap, we have no idea whether we will make it across" (Scharmer O., 2015, p. 25). According to Rohr, the message of the medieval Christian text *The Cloud of Unknowing* is: "The spiritual journey demands full self-awareness and honesty, a perpetual shadow-boxing with our own weaknesses and imperfections. While physical withdrawal from the world is not essential, letting go of attachments to people, expectations, and things is. This requires contemplative practice, a true spiritual discipline. Rather than teaching passivity, the path into the cloud of unknowing requires active intent, willingness, and practice — knowing enough to not need to know more, which ironically becomes a kind of endless, deeper knowing" (Rohr, 2015). The significance of both accounts is their illustration of letting go as a gateway to freedom defined as the ability to surrender to where an action or decision takes you. To Isaac Pennington it meant: "Give over thine own willing, give over thy own running, give over thine own desiring to know or be anything and sink down to the seed which God sows in the heart, and let that grow in thee and be in thee and breathe in thee and act in thee" (QFP, para. 26.70).

- Theory U, however, can be understood at many levels. At one level, Theory U acts like a compass helping discerners keep on track. For Brent Bill: "A compass, no matter what direction we turn, always points to the north pole … In that way, a compass makes a good metaphor for our spiritual lives and the work of discerning God's will for us … the divine compass points us to our spiritual true north – the mind and love of God …" (Bill, 2008, p. xi). At a deeper level, the U map is a gateway to the inner journey of discernment. My enquiry adapts it to explore and enrich our inner perception of Quaker discernment.

- I liken exploring the U and Theory U to going on a walk taking a map with a marked route and having a GPS tracker on my phone. Arthur's three movements (see diagrams 1-3) are equivalent to a national road map – at this scale all it shows is the basic shape of a journey. When I zoom into the finer detail – the fuller Theory U map (see diagram 4) – I begin to mark a route that shows the direction of my journey and the main stages to note as I pass through. When I do the walk and track GPS waypoints, the line of the track I actually walk is much more winding and complex than the route appears to be. I may not actually pass through the stages as described. I might by-pass one. I might double back on myself before finding my way forward. I may take some mini-deviations from the route! But if I lose my way, I need the route to check my location compared to where I need to be in order to find my direction again. I argue that turning to Quaker discernment is like picking up another map of the same area; the principal features are still there, but the colours and style are different.

- Drawing on Theory U I note four principal strands in making decisions that emerge from inner knowing. These are underpinning themes in exploring Quaker discernment as making decisions for the best:

  * *Opening* of mind, heart and will to support a central purpose of

  * *Resting* in the deepest inner place or source I can access thus allowing inner knowing to emerge. This is dependent on

  * *Listening* to distinguish between the many voices that are 'heard'. Listening is more than aural listening and includes a wide range of different ways of 'listening' and

  * *Paying attention* to the inner place from which I – and a group – operate.

Chapter 3. Quaker Discernment

In Philip Pullman's novel *Northern Lights*, Lyra is given an alethiometer because "it tells you the truth ... as for how to read it, you'll have to learn by yourself as it is a symbol reader" (Pullman, 1995). Quaker discernment is a little like this. Discernment is the alethiometer but we each have to learn how to practise it and become familiar with the way we each read the symbols that are our promptings and insight. Nevertheless, its importance is clear from this extract from the Epistle from Britain Yearly Meeting in 2013:

"Discernment is a discipline; it requires time, effort, trust, and practice. To engage in it fully, we need to let go of our own notions and preconceptions and pray with humility, 'not my will but thine be done'. In a culture that values speed and efficiency, our Quaker methods may seem slow, but they enable us to listen to and follow the guidance of the Spirit. Do we exercise enough patience and resist our desire for easy answers? Patient listening eventually leads to a feeling of rightness as a decision is reached; bringing our uncertainties into the presence of God is part of the search for truth."

Compiling an account of Quaker discernment

I find no single account of Quaker discernment, what it is and how it is done. Thus the account that follows is compiled from a variety of sources and I rely primarily on the literature review that I undertook as part of my research. My account relies extensively on secondary sources selected from books, pamphlets and articles for discernment courses at Woodbrooke Quaker Study Centre. I also draw on a limited amount of primary research from reflections and observations made by participants on courses on discernment and on decision-making in Quaker-led organisations. I also had access to material from an exploratory session on concern, individual and corporate discernment (SE Scotland Area Quaker Meeting, 2016) in the form of notes shared with me by Michael Hutchinson, who led the session (Hutchinson, 2016) and post-it notes by participants in response to his questions.

Earlier I quoted Brian Arthur observing: "For the big decisions in life, you need to reach a deeper region of consciousness. Making decisions then becomes not so much about 'deciding' as about letting an inner wisdom emerge" (Jaworski, 2012, pp. 310/3302, Kindle). Spirit-led discernment holds that the source of this inner knowing is God and its purpose is to discover and follow the will of God. A common theme in Quaker practice and Theory U is that both challenge the prevailing view of decision-making as an analytical process carried out by separated minds. Rational analysis has an important part to play in discernment but it is in informing discernment not the means by which the actual discernment is made.

Developing discernment 'muscles' and Ignatian discernment

The purpose of discernment in Christian religious traditions is seeking to be guided by God. Our human anxiety is wondering what God may ask of us, no doubt remembering that for Jesus "not my will but thine" led to death. Lonsdale describes the will of God as more like God's hopes and desires, thus the will of God is akin to harmonising with God's music, or being freed to dance to the music of creation – dancing one's own steps but finding you are dancing in unison with God's dance (Lonsdale, 1992).

In the Christian tradition, discernment is an on-going practice in daily life as well as formal processes of communal discernment. One source observes: "In classical spirituality, discernment means distinguishing God's Spirit from other spirits that are present in a given time and place – such as the spirit of a nation, the spirit of the times, or the spirit of competition. To put it another way, discernment is distinguishing the voice of God from other voices that speak to us: the voice of our parents speaking echoing from years past, the voices of friends, of urgency or fear. These voices are neither bad nor good in and of themselves. God often speaks to us through them. But, if followed indiscriminately, such voices can dominate us and lead us along a wrong path" (Farnham, et al., 1996, p. 6). Quaker *Advices & Queries* express this simply as: "Be aware of the spirit of God at work in the ordinary activities and experience of your daily life" (QFP, 2016, para 1.02.7). This is the material for 'little discernings' through which we learn to read the symbols of our own discernment alethiometer, nurtured by time set aside for personal inward reflection. Such regular training of our individual discernment muscles through personal discernment is the ground upon which collective or corporate discernment rests: "We can only expect discernment to be achieved in major matters if we have practised sufficiently on a smaller scale, so that this faculty is exercised, and so that we are familiar with its workings. Taking heed to the very small promptings and seeing where they lead, what feelings and thoughts and experience follow when they are obeyed, or when they are ignored, will help us to develop this part of ourselves as we do any other" (Heathfield, 1994, p 26).

Discernment has always been important in the Ignatian community, fostered in a series of steps. The clarity with which they lay them out is a helpful template.

- Prayer,

- Adequate information that helps the group consider what is the greatest need, the mission, options and resources available to this,

- Spiritual freedom – being genuinely free to follow the discerned decision, releasing any preference for one outcome over another,

- Occasionally through dramatic circumstance or an epiphany – St Paul's conversion experience on the road to Damascus is an example,

- Through feeling – affective discernment – where consolation and desolation are touchstones of the individual's relationship with God in the matter being discerned. Thus consolations are feelings such as joy, peace, happiness, confidence, and love marking that the discernment decision is drawing closer to God and desolations might be marked by anger, resentment, resistance, envy and guilt as signs of turning away from God,

- By weighing the reasons – such as identifying the decision options and systematically listing the pros and cons of each, then

- Discernment is confirmed in response to sifting and sorting, sitting in prayer with the matter and noting whether responses confirm a decision or indicate further searching is needed,

- The discernment continues through shared discussion until it becomes clear that all concerned are agreed on the way forward,

- Discernment emerges at the point when individual discernments are aligned – the will of God is perceived as the presence of the Holy Spirit marked in coming together in consensus.

From this summary of Ignatian discernment as a prominent example of spirit-led discernment, I now turn specifically on Quaker discernment.

Quaker discernment

A paragraph in *Quaker Faith & Practice* (QFP), the authoritative source on the Quaker way as practised in Britain, states: "Discernment and decision-making are crucial aspects of our life as a Quaker community" (QFP, 2016, para. 8.02). Yet I found no comprehensive account of discernment in QFP nor does a search on the main Quakers in Britain website[6] offer an overview of this aspect of life as a Quaker community. The online edition (QFP, 2016) contains fifty-two references to 'discern' or 'discernment'. In general, they are used to show Quakers' particular and careful manner of working together, considering matters and making decisions – Quakers do not on the whole just 'decide' or 'agree'. Only some dozen references explicitly describe *what* discernment is or *how* to discern. Nevertheless, a summary of Quaker discernment can be compiled from QFP (para reference after each extract):

- *Its importance*: "Discernment and decision-making are crucial aspects of our life as a Quaker community" (8.02) … "as discerned by the gathered meeting, or the Inward Word of God in our hearts which is available to each of us who seek the Truth" (29.17);

- *Being discerning*: "A common purpose in seeking God's will through waiting and listening, believing that every activity of life should be subject to divine guidance" (3.02);

- *Equality in respect for each member of the community*: "I believe that it is that uniqueness that above all needs to be cherished, protected, nourished and helped to grow and flower and come to fruition. Our job is to discern and to promote this uniqueness" (21.36) … "Our ability to discern the gifts of others is not perfect and we will recognise an element of God's grace in our deliberations" (3.25);

- *Equality of responsibility*: "All of us have a part to play in the processes of discernment leading to decisions [on spending money] on the work to be undertaken" (14.07);

---

[6] www.quaker.org.uk/

- *Drawing on Quaker business method as a template for Quaker discernment*: "Help Friends to remember that the period of silent worship at the beginning of the meeting prepares for and opens the way to the consideration of the business" (3.13) … "all coming to them in an active, seeking spirit, not with minds already made up on a particular course of action, determined to push this through at all costs" (3.05);

- *Opening minds*: "But open minds are not empty minds, nor uncritically receptive: the service of the meeting calls for knowledge of facts, often painstakingly acquired, and the ability to estimate their relevance and importance." (3.05) … "Provide sufficient background information to set the meeting purposefully on its course" (3.13);

- *Opening hearts*: "This demands that we shall be ready to listen to others carefully, without antagonism if they express opinions which are unpleasing to us, but trying always to discern the truth in what they have to offer. It calls, above all, for spiritual sensitivity. If our meetings fail, the failure may well be in those who are ill-prepared to use the method rather than in the inadequacy of the method itself" (3.05);

- *Opening the will*: "Expectation that God's guidance can be discerned if we are truly listening together and to each other, and are not blinkered by preconceived opinions" (3.02) … "be sensitive to discern things with fairness and unaffected by prejudice. I felt the need to be faithful to truth instead of relying on existing judgment." (24.16) … "What is required is a willingness to listen to what others have to say rather than to persuade them that one's own point of view represents what is right and proper. It also requires restraint. The reiteration of one point by several Friends each in their own way lends no weight to the point. What the meeting must learn to discern is its rightness, not how many people support it …" (2.90);

- *Clerking and discernment*: "The meeting places upon its clerk a responsibility for spiritual discernment so that he or she may watch the growth of the meeting toward unity and judge the right time to submit the minute, which in its first form may serve to clear the mind of the meeting about the issues which really need its decision. In a gathering held 'in the life' there can come to the clerk a clear and unmistakeable certainty about the moment to submit the minute." (3.07);

- *Discernment is mediated through our humanness*: "Friends should realise that a decision which is the only one for a particular meeting at a particular time may not be the one which is ultimately seen to be right." (3.07);

- *A tempo to Quaker discernment*: "It is this belief that God's will can be recognised through the discipline of silent waiting which distinguishes our decision-making process from the secular idea of consensus." (3.02) ... "When conflict comes, as it does, and the temptation to compromise – to seek consensus – is resisted, the sense of divine guidance is unmistakably registered. New possibilities for a way forward which nobody has thought of emerge out of discussion. Postponement and delay settle minds and assist the process of coming to a united mind" (2.90).

... And illustrated further

Three further quotations amplify this summary and confirm its foundational and holistic place in Quaker spirituality:

- Quaker discernment is "central to Quaker practice, a practice of waiting and deep listening that filters out distractions and 'noise' to reach clarity guided by the promptings of Love and Truth" (QSA, 2013, p. 3, footnote).

- Parker Palmer (Palmer, 2004), a noted contemporary Quaker writer, teacher and retreat leader in the US, says he was attracted to Quakerism by its two pillars: "the conviction that every human being has direct inward access to God, and the equally strong conviction that we need a community of discernment to help us sort and sift what we think we are hearing from within. As depth psychology and good theology remind us – and as many of us know from experience – not every voice from within is the voice of God" (Farnham, et al., 2011, p. xiv).

- Roy Stephenson, explains discernment as "to seek for Truth to live by, this deep listening for Divine wisdom, we call discernment. We must listen for the Inward Teacher ... Our human nature is an important tool, for discernment involves empathy, realism and imagination, and also good hard thought about how to move from the way things are to how they could be. But it also involves stepping outside of ourselves, moving away from 'this is what I think' to 'what this situation needs?' For me this is a form of prayer, because it means putting oneself in a place where one tries to see things with God's eyes – though it's not what's conventionally considered to be prayer" (Stephenson, 2013).

The language of God in Quaker discernment

Any discussion of Quaker discernment quickly encounters a range of assumptions, understanding and language associated with God amongst Quakers. Historically, Quakers draw strongly on the experience of early Quakers whose natural language and understanding of life was primarily God-centred. However, what early Quakers believed about the nature of God was often unorthodox for its time and extended beyond conventional images of God as a white male figure in the sky.

Early Quakers write about God as the spirit of Christ, as the source of the inner teacher, inward light or seed that prompts the search for love and the God within. On the basis of her recent research Anne Adams argues that early Quaker spirituality went further and embraced the whole of creation, bringing a "sense of security but also [of] awareness and feeling of being in touch with the cosmos, responsible for one's part in its evolution". She goes on to argue this vision was later lost in more human-centred Quaker testimonies to justice, peace, integrity, simplicity, truth and equality (Adams, 2012, p. 34). Rex Ambler's research into the Inward Light of early Quakers found it to be a Light you see by, like the light of the sun; "it enabled you to become aware of the reality around you, and indeed of the reality inside you, but which you could not normally see because of the dark … Fox's message was new and startling. He was telling people they had the Light of God within them and that, if they could open themselves to it, it would show them all they needed to know" (Ambler, 2013, p.6). Ambler suggests that Quakers' original perception of the Inward Light was of a capacity for awareness in every human being; the Light was revealed first as self-awareness, and it revealed the source of Light and unity (Ambler, 2013).

This diversity of understanding is threaded through Quaker writing. Some of the following passages from *Quaker Faith & Practice* (QFP, 2016) use more customary language whilst others allude to an intangible sense of the divine. The extracts give a snapshot of the kind of meanings Quakers use about the source from which they act and Quaker inner knowing, e.g.

- "Worship is the response of the human spirit to the presence of the divine and eternal, to the God who first seeks us." (QFP, 2016, para 2.01);

- "Bring the whole of your life under the ordering of the spirit of Christ ... Cherish that of God within you, so that this love may grow in you and guide you." (QFP, 2016, para 1.02.2);

- "In silence which is active, the Inner Light begins to glow – a tiny spark. For the flame to be kindled and to grow, subtle argument and the clamour of our emotions must be stilled. It is by an attention full of love that we enable the Inner Light to blaze and illuminate our dwelling and to make of our whole being a source from which this Light may shine out." (QFP, 2016, para 21.12);

- "In our meetings for worship we seek through the stillness to know God's will for ourselves and for the gathered group. Our meetings for church affairs, in which we conduct our business, are also meetings for worship based on silence, and they carry the same expectation that God's guidance can be discerned if we are truly listening together and to each other, and are not blinkered by preconceived opinions. It is this belief that God's will can be recognised through the discipline of silent waiting which distinguishes our decision-making process from the secular idea of consensus. We have a common purpose in seeking God's will through waiting and listening, believing that every activity of life should be subject to divine guidance." (QFP, 2016, para 3.02);

- "All of us need to find a way into silence which allows us to deepen our awareness of the divine and to find the inward source of our strength." (QFP, 2016, para 1.02.3).

Although not directly used in relation to discernment, Quakers often speak of "that of God" and this offers a nuanced perception of relationship to God and it is helpful for many in thinking about the language of Quaker discernment.

Quaker language and discernment

Jo Farrow, a British Quaker writing about discernment in the Quaker tradition, wrote that the Quaker movement developed at a time when religious movements echoed "a period of intense speculation and excitement about the place of the Holy Spirit in the ordering of Church life". She points out that: "The Society of Friends has been described by one of its historians as a 'holy experiment in spiritual guidance'." Farrow suggests that if Quaker meetings were in any way a holy experiment or 'laboratories of the Spirit', as Steere called them (Steere, 2005, p. 15), then this was true in so far as Quaker meetings were "a space in which Friends can explore the meaning of holy obedience and test their findings in a process which involves every member of the meeting in the exercise of corporate discernment" (Farrow, 1989, pp. 51-52, 60).

Perhaps as a consequence, Quakers give particular meaning to a range of words and short phrases, almost a special language, that illustrate how Quakers experience discernment, e.g.: leadings, nudges, prompting, quieting, waiting, listening, hearing, clearness, opening, threshing, sense of the meeting, reaching unity, testing. I have put them in this order as in a nutshell they hint at the sequence of Quaker discernment. The manner of Quaker discernment is generally (but not always) reflective, quiet and involves sinking down into oneself. The purpose of waiting is to allow time to listen, for a clear leading to grow; it is not instant like turning on a tap. At the same time, practised skilfully, it feels well-grounded, and is done with intent and in a reverential manner.

The subjective nature of inner motions such as openings, leadings, nudges and promptings led the first generation of Quakers to put structures in place to test individual discernment in the community. There had been a few, but notable, occasions when individual discernment was acted upon and brought Quakers into disrepute; testing it in community was a check on this. Waiting was part of the test of an authentic call, and listening was a key practice, both inwardly to God and outwardly with the Quaker community or meeting. Farrow's interpretation is that: "In order to survive as a cohesive group Friends accepted a minimal hierarchical structure and carefully formulated guidelines for the conduct of meetings" and the combination of "the ethical demand, the inward wrestling, and the way found to move forward in obedience" (Farrow, 1989, pp. 59-60).

This blend of individual and communal continues. Benefiel describes their interdependence: "Spiritual discernment is practiced both individually and corporately. Even when done individually, it is never in isolation. Individual and corporate discernment dance together, hand in hand. Corporate discernment requires prepared hearts and minds of the individuals involved. Individual discernment requires the support of a community, nurturing and grounding the person's spiritual life. Individual discernment also requires the accountability of a community, offering checks and balances to the individual's discernment" (Benefiel, 2005, Loc 829/2706, Kindle). The whole comprises a gestalt (a whole that is perceived as more than the sum of its parts) that gives Quaker discernment considerable depth and integrity. However, numerous Quaker Meetings and organisations struggle with consistently good practice or skilful discernment.

Accounts of Quaker and spirit-led discernment

I turn next to a number of accounts of Quaker discernment that together illustrate Benefiel's view of "a process of going deeper. It is drawing on one's whole self, heart, mind, soul and spirit … it is the bringing together of all one's faculties within the larger context of the transcendent" (Benefiel, 2005, p. 51). They also illustrate Lyra's observation that you learn to read the symbols of your alethiometer.

Peter Eccles

A process of going deeper is borne out in Peter Eccles' exploration of discernment in *The Presence in the Midst*. Eccles has clerked[7] Britain Yearly Meeting[8], amongst other corporate bodies, and he draws on a wealth of experience of individual and corporate discernment. Eccles sees God as a Spirit "an all-pervasive creative force at work in the universe". He cites a reference by Pierre de Chardin to "the within of things" as: "Everything has an inner

---

[7] A role that combines responsibility for the conduct of the meeting with discerning when those present are reaching unity about their response to a matter and recording a minute that group agrees expresses that unity.
[8] The annual meeting of Quakers in Britain

element of spiritual energy which lies dormant until it is set in motion by the increasing chemical complexity of the beginnings of life; then there is a sudden change of state with the appearance of self-awareness. Our self-awareness also appears to bring with it a growing spiritual awareness: an awareness of truth, of good and of beauty; of the all-pervasive creative force at work in the universe, which is God" (Eccles, 2009, p. 52).

Reflecting on his day-by-day experience, Eccles writes: "There is a sense in which I can always be aware of the Spirit at work within me and of an inner stillness available to me" (Eccles, 2009, p. 82) and shares that, nevertheless, he is uncomfortable with the idea that "God wills us to take a particular course of action; ... when we talk about 'seeking the will of God' I understand this as indicating the importance we attach to a decision and also the importance we attach to the way we make the decision. If we understand God as a constructive creative force in the universe, then 'seeking the will of God' or 'praying to be rightly led' describe a process in which we seek so to align ourselves with the creative force we call God that the decisions we make are constructive and creative. Inspiration may come from outside us, from other people or from inner experience, but in the end the decision is ours." He continues with a brief experiential description as he adds: "As I pray for guidance in writing this lecture I do not imagine that God has a text ready for me to discover. However, I do believe that there are words that are true to my experience and appropriate for the purpose; if I am centred and open to God's leadings then I will be helped to find these words" (Eccles, 2009, p. 86).

In determining personal choices Eccles likens discernment to finding a route up a mountain: "The criterion for the acceptability of a route is that it follows the rules of the Spirit, the way of Truth ... sometimes you just seem to know that a route is right." As a mathematician he likens his awareness of the testing of discernment to solving a mathematical problem: "On occasion everything suddenly falls into place ... You know that it is right before you have even checked all the details ... Just as in mathematics, we have to remember that a moment of apparent clarity can sometimes be misguided; we must always be retesting our lifetime decisions." His perspective widens to global issues – stewardship of the earth's resources and conflict resolution – and offers a view that "I don't believe that God has a prepared 'model solution' to these problems, but God's guidance, or the leadings of the Spirit, provide us with the means to seek a creative response and assess our own efforts. We may not be able to solve these dilemmas but we can seek to contribute to the solution" (Eccles, 2009, pp. 89-90).

To round out this overview, I turn to three American writers, and a further British voice who offer varying but congruent pictures of discernment: Patricia Loring is an American Quaker whose books on *Listening Spirituality* present a wide range of tools for reflective listening; Nancy Bieber, a spiritual director, psychologist, retreat leader and Quaker, author of *Decision Making and Spiritual Discernment* teaches in an ecumenical setting; and Elizabeth Liebert, author of *The Way of Discernment* and *The Soul of Discernment*, Professor of Spiritual Life at San Francisco Theological Seminary and a Roman Catholic sister drawing on twenty-five years of leading discernment retreats. The British voice is Michael Hutchinson who retired in 2013 after many years' service as assistant recording clerk of Britain Yearly Meeting thus gathering a wealth of experience from observation and practice.

Patricia Loring

Patricia Loring calls her major work "listening spirituality" and makes it clear that, from her point of view, discernment "is the 'heart' of listening ... and the heart of Quaker spirituality". She explains it as a process that focuses on "our individual and corporate ability to discern, distinguish or sift Divine Guidance from other promptings ... Quaker spirituality demands of us a commitment to a much more subtle and strenuous effort to discriminate movements of the Spirit among the complex motivations, forces and dimensions of experience within and around us" (Loring, 1999, pp. 67-68). It is rooted in listening, as Loring explains: "By listening I mean the widest kind of prayerful, discerning attentiveness to the Source intimated within us, evidenced through others, and discernible through the experiences of life. This kind of listening is not simply auditory. It may be visual, kinesthetic, intuitive or visceral as well, depending on the deepest attentiveness natural to the individual" (Loring, 1997, p. 2). The point of such listening is that it "opens us to transformation by the Spirit of God" (Loring, 1997, p. 6). She, like Eccles, points out that Quaker listening spirituality, unguided by dogma, catechism or liturgy, makes us more reliant on our capacity to accurately discern divine guidance from other promptings.

In an earlier pamphlet, Loring spelt out some key characteristics of discernment. The five extracts below come from the introduction to the pamphlet. They are arranged to show a sequence of key elements in a discernment cycle (pamphlet page reference given alongside each point) (Loring, 1992):

- "Discernment is the faculty we use to distinguish the true movement of the Spirit. It's grounded in the central Quaker conviction of the availability to every person of the experience and guidance of God, immediate as well as mediated" … "[it] is a gift from God, not a personal achievement. The gift is not the result of training, technique, or analysis." (p3);

- "Friends have not been unaware that an interior spirituality without exterior checks carries risks. While affirming that of God in every person, they have been well aware that there is that of a great many other things in every person as well – the 'creaturely' tendencies to egocentricity and self-will are two" – "not distinguishing between a motion of the spirit and the most pressing or plausible impulse within themselves" (p4);

- "One by one we move beyond conceptions of our selves … on the way to unmediated, unknowing, intimate relationship with the Source of our being. This via negativa into ourselves overlaps part of the terrain we travel on the via negativa to God." (p 15);

- "…trust increasingly that prompting and leadings of the Spirit will show us the way we are to go" (p4) "…faithfulness required thinking through whether and how leadings (decisions) might be authenticated" (p4).

Loring also argues that discernment was experienced differently in earlier times compared to now. She says that amongst earlier Friends the response to "inward prompting was experienced as obedience to the requirements of a transcendent, yet utterly present, deity" (Loring, 1999, p. 68). In contrast, what arose during the twentieth century, she says, "has often been felt more nearly as cooperation – sometimes articulated as co-creation – with God." Loring then explains co-creation in a way that is congruent with an emerging inner knowing: "Co-creation implies a still unfolding creation in which the Creator continues to work with and through us when we respond in faithfulness to the promptings of Love and Truth in our hearts" (Loring, 1999, p. 69).

Nancy Bieber

At the beginning of my enquiry, I described three different ways that the word discernment is used. The first of these – being discerning – constitutes a considered way in which a decision is made, how an individual or group holds itself accountable and the practice used to achieve this; Bieber's work offers a clear, practical guide to discernment and comprehensive examples of this kind of being discerning as spirit-led. She uses the image of three strands, or braids, of willingness, attentiveness and responsiveness. She says that over the years during which she has gathered her experience, the three strands "weave together again and again, creating a strong rope to grasp on to, a clear practice for managing life decisions" (Bieber, 2011, p. 6). Although the strands have to be described sequentially, their depth and resilience comes from the way that each acts on and with the others to make discernment a strong braid in daily practice.

Bieber introduces her approach to discernment with an inclusive overview of making decisions. She says it is inherently sacred work as: "Through our decisions, we shape our unique and sacred lives … it will flow more smoothly when we recognize it as a sacred process, and are willing to allow the Spirit to illuminate our decision-making" and that "When we open all our decisions to the Spirit, we learn to see more clearly what is true and real" (Bieber, 2011, p. 5). What I note in these remarks is how different in tone this is from exhortations to follow the will of God. Bieber relates discernment to the sacredness of our lives and honouring the importance of our decisions by opening to wisdom and love to help us see more clearly what is true and real. It seems to me this places the individual discerner at the centre, turning to a source of inner knowing and engaging in a co-creative relationship with Spirit.

Similarly, her discussion of the source of our discernment is helpful in enlarging our point of reference when making a decision for the best: "Although God is at the center of our decision-making, we all come with unique understandings about God" and of the many names for God "all of them are attempts to describe something that is larger than any names". Among her favourite names for God are

Spirit, Love, Guide, Light and "One of my favourite names for God is the one I learned from author and teacher Tilden Edwards: Something More." She continues: "Perhaps the God name that is most helpful for spiritual discernment is Light ... [she refers to words for God from different religious traditions] ... My Quaker tradition uses light as a metaphor for the transcendent God and describes that which is of God within us as the inner Light" (Bieber, 2011, p. 9).

On discernment, she says simply yet clearly: "When we make a decision, even a small one, it expresses something about our fundamental values. We make decisions according to what gives meaning and worth to our lives." In her understanding, discernment is made by reference to our wish to make good decisions, to shape our lives well and choose carefully and wisely. Bieber recognises fears about being willing to open to Spirit. Such fear "tends to expand beyond its [protective] boundaries and to outlive its usefulness". She approaches our experience of fear sympathetically; it leads us to hold on tightly, to be apprehensive, thus limiting our choices and giving fear too much power over us. She says that noticing fear can have important things to tell us if we listen: "Significant life stories are contained within them. These stories still shape our lives, and, unless we pay attention to them, we won't know if the way they shape us is helpful or not" (Bieber, 2011, pp. 31-32). Respect for ourselves and challenging our inner processes is a hallmark of Bieber's spiritual discernment. She argues that we must respect fear in order to interrogate it: "Who are you? What are you about? Where do you come from? Can we talk?"

To this end "we need something to help us step forward" which, for Bieber, means "we need the aid of that wise and loving Spirit whose wisdom and light exceed our own" (Bieber, 2011, pp. 4-5). In later passages Bieber raises the question of our willingness to relinquish control: "But saying 'yes' is opening to wisdom beyond the mind's own. This willingness seems to access the kind of knowing we call intuitive. The reasoning mind's analytical ability needs to open to God's wisdom so it can honor the more subtle knowing of intuitive wisdom" (Bieber, 2011, p. 22). Moreover, Bieber recounts this connection with God's wisdom as a deeply heartfelt experience: "The heart's experience of 'yes' lies in the feelings we have when we open to God. We have ached for connection to something more ... So our heart's 'yes' comes with feelings of gladness and joy. There can be a deep relief at having something besides ourselves to help us find our way through the confusing decisions and conflicting choices of daily life." And, continuing in words that echo my next writer, Elizabeth Liebert, Bieber reports: "Embracing that [yes] is liberating and freeing." Whereas a number of Bieber's observations imply we alone are unable to provide the inner knowing we need, she also says that opening to Something More may feel risky: "Trusting another, even God, can make us feel vulnerable. Even when we consider ourselves co-creators with God, we might be worried about the One we're collaborating with" (Bieber, 2011, pp. 22-23).

This passage alerts us to an aspect of Bieber's perspective of discernment that Loring also addresses clearly in the passage above – that opening to Something More brings us into co-creative relationship with an unfolding creation. Opening our will, in particular, enables us to become the hands that respond to promptings of love and truth. If decisions for the best are to be from the whole and for the whole, we need to be able to trust being in relationship with wisdom and light.

Elizabeth Liebert

Liebert, like the other writers quoted, characterises spirit-led discernment as guidance in our daily decisions "... to help you listen, notice, discriminate, and choose within your own relationship to the One who ultimately sustains the whole world" (Liebert, 2011, p. xiii). She cites it as possibly the single most important Christian spiritual practice for addressing: "How are we to live our lives thoughtfully and faithfully in the midst of all the forces, options, and decisions that characterize modern life? ... What if we understood these decisions, minor as well as major, as a matter of faithful Christian living?" (Liebert, 2008, p. ix) She links a practice of discernment to our personal and spiritual growth: "Discernment is the process of intentionally becoming aware of how God is present, active and calling us as individuals and communities so we can respond with increasingly greater faithfulness" and more specifically "Because our identity is formed in part through our decisions, the making of decisions is actually a privileged moment for growing into discipleship. Through our choices, we can become the person God is calling us to be" (Liebert, 2008, p. 8 & 7). For Liebert, discernment has a more clear-cut Christian aspect than for Loring or Bieber: "We gradually put on the mind of Christ every time we search out and choose that which better aligns us with the Jesus of the Gospels, the Christ of faith. A discerning life, then, is composed of repeating discerning moments ... Our intention is that all our decisions will enhance this putting on the mind of Christ" (Liebert, 2008, pp. 9-10).

Michael Hutchinson

My final voice of spirit-led discernment illustrates one further view of Quaker discernment. It is compiled from two sources: notes from a talk given by Michael Hutchinson when he led a workshop on concern and discernment for South East Scotland Area Quaker Meeting in February 2016 and post-it notes that collate participants' response to activities that were part of the workshop. The words Hutchinson uses to describe discernment bear witness to an unfolding and organic process (I re-organise the order of the notes to follow something more like the three movements through a U process). Initially Hutchinson describes the careful nature of a discernment process: "recognising, sifting, threshing, discussion, separating sheep from goats, clarify, questioning, teasing out, sharing, exploring, working out". Hutchinson describes a process that slows as it is more deeply considered and suggests it is a Quaker 'art': "giving time, stepping back, discretion, insight, openness, thoughtfulness". There is further deepening and slowing – centring down perhaps – as he uses words such as "empathy, prayerful thought, clarity, stillness, listening, light awareness, deep, spiritual, sensitive, weighing, reflection, care, spirit in room" until it reaches "silent waiting, sitting in the light, seeking for guidance, quiet, together, [corporate] listening, prayer". He weighs the process by its fruits, not of the Spirit exactly as they appear in Paul's letter to the Galatians – love, joy, peace, patience, kindness, goodness, faithfulness, gentleness, and self-control – but more as outcomes: "feeling of rightness, a decision, unity, commitment, long-term, joint/mutual, priorities, energy" (Hutchinson, 2016).

Reflections: an overview of general principles of Quaker discernment

• At the end of the previous chapter on Theory U I identified four key strands in discernment:

* *Opening* of mind, heart and will to support a central purpose of

* *Resting* in the deepest inner place or source I can access thus allowing inner knowing to emerge. This is dependent on

* *Listening* to distinguish between the many voices that are 'heard' and

* *Paying attention* to the inner place from which I – and a group – operate.

I note all four strands can be observed in the extracts above that illustrate Quaker discernment. The extracts from *Quaker Faith & Practice* illustrate this quite clearly as do the other extracts in differing ways. The accounts vary as each writer offers a different perspective on discernment. It's a little like each one is feeling an elephant – knowing it is the same elephant – but finding different words, and images to convey the nature of the elephant to those less familiar with elephants.

* Above all, it seems to me the extracts suggest that the integrity of Quaker discernment rests on the way in which the Quaker community creates a culture of discernment. Its ongoing strength is likely to depend on the degree and stability with which it successfully upholds this. A culture of Quaker discernment is clearly signposted in the extracts from British Quaker voices, both *Quaker Faith & Practice* and the individual narratives from Eccles and Hutchinson. The culture of discernment rests on shared values (e.g. respect, equality), behaviours (e.g. listening, waiting), attitudes (e.g. active, seeking spirit, acceptance) and practices (e.g. knowledge of facts, discern gifts), and these show up clearly in the accounts by Eccles and Hutchinson.

* *Opening whether of mind, heart and will* is associated with confronting those factors that limit and block our capacity to act for the best. This is shown in the extracts from Parker Palmer, Eccles, and Loring, as well as Bieber and Liebert. There is evidence of consciously setting aside preconceived ideas and baggage, putting those aside in favour of what is best for the issue not best for our own interests. Loring speaks of complex motivations and the strand of opening is evident in the quotes from her pamphlet. Bieber gives attention to fear, such as fear of not being in charge,

fear of change, fear of trusting the guide and, indeed, fear that the God of our imagination may not actually be there; in this instance Bieber observes that, like Puddleglum in *The Silver Chair,* we can choose to act as if God is real even though we can't be certain. She highlights a paradox: "The evidence of God's creative love, presence and activity in the world actually depends on us trusting in God and stepping out ourselves. It lies in our taking the risk when we don't know how it will turn out" (Bieber, 2011, pp. 39-40). Parker Palmer highlights opening being upheld through the need for a community of discernment to help us. Quaker communities themselves provide a route to opening, helping us sort and sift what we think we are hearing. Interestingly, Eccles hints that in his experience a source of opening is connected with help to find the words as he writes and recognising that he can be misled. It seems to me that opening is deeply ingrained in Quaker discernment and is an organic part of the culture. Indeed, the first chapter of *Quaker Faith & Practice* reads in part: "Do not allow the strength of your convictions to betray you into making statements or allegations that are unfair or untrue. Think it possible that you may be mistaken" (QFP, 2016, para. 1.02).

- The second element – *a purpose of allowing an inner wisdom to emerge* – is central to numerous accounts in which inner knowing is encountered as wisdom and love, and in some accounts named as God. Nevertheless, the Quaker writers explored above interpret the nature of the source of inner knowing in various ways. Eccles speaks of an all-pervading creative force at work in the universe whilst being at ease with the language of God; being led is seeking to align ourselves with the creative force we call God. Loring refers to God throughout, yet she makes it clear that she perceives this as an unfolding creation and a Creator that works with us, which we register as the promptings of Love and Truth. Loring's God is a responsive yet not directive figure. Bieber's approach is sensitive to the range of perceptions amongst her audience – she writes of "your own relationship to the One who ultimately sustains the whole world" – whilst pointing toward a wise and loving Spirit. There is a recognisable principle in Quakerism of recognising and answering "that of God" in everyone; each of the writers I explore above explains what source is to them in ways that sit within this loose frame.

- The third and fourth strands in my enquiry – developing outward and inward *listening* and *paying attention* to the inner place from which we operate – are considered by each of the writers above. I consider these strands further in later chapters.

I began this chapter by likening the various accounts of Quaker discernment to an alethiometer, which leaves much to the discerner to learn how to read the symbols. I conclude my account of Quaker discernment with two linked diagrams (see below and next page) that represent a first step in capturing Quaker discernment through the flow of a U map. The first is an acrostic developed by Vera Dolton in which the letters of the word 'discernment' can be read vertically, and the associated steps in discernment are explained horizontally alongside each letter. In the second diagram, I show how these steps might translate into a U map of Quaker discernment. The variety of steps in the 'acrostic' and map show discernment as a rich process of steps with mini choices on the way. It is not just coming to stillness, listening, accessing inner knowing and then acting.

Diagram 8: An overview of discernment – an acrostic

DISCERNMENT
In a spirit of prayerfulness throughout

Data-base	What do I know now?
Information	Gathering what I need
Sifting and sorting	Ready for use
Consultation	How does it look to others - what help and/or support can they give?
Examination and evaluation	How does it look so far? Have I done all I can?
Reflection - turning it over	How does it FEEL?
Nothing - whenever possible, wait	Leave - then review - 'listen' to self and God
Make decision	In the light of the above
Execute	Act on decision
Nurture	Give it the best chance
Test	In due course, evaluate the process, the decision, the outcome, your feelings

Diagram 9: Incorporating the Discernment acrostic into a Quaker U map

Downloading – the 'database': what do I know at the start of a discernment
SUSPENDING

Seeing: with fresh eyes, Gathering information. Sifting, sorting ready for use

REDIRECTING

Feeling: listening to others – consultation, reflection, other points of view – how does it feel?

LETTING GO:
Pause and review

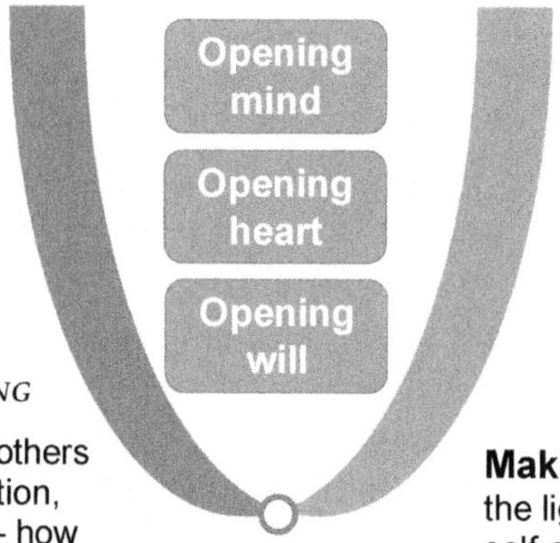

Opening mind

Opening heart

Opening will

Performing - test. In due course evaluate the process, the decision, the outcome, your feelings

EMBODYING
Prototyping Execute. Nurture. Give it the best chance.

ENACTING

Making a decision in the light of listening to self and God

LETTING COME:
Reflect and wait

Presencing – listen to self and God

Chapter 4. Going Down: Weaving Theory U and Quaker Discernment

In 1971, Douglas Steere and his wife visited India and Japan. It was a landmark moment for him as they intentionally opened themselves to Hinduism and Zen Buddhism, "seeking to discern the message of each, and its relevance to the Christian life of the spirit". From this Steere observed: "Something happens in the course of understanding another's truth that irradiates and lights up one's own tradition and that on rare occasions may even give one a hint of a truth that embraces both, a hint of a hidden convergence" (Steere, 1971, p. 7). He called this 'mutual irradiation'.

The mutual irradiation described above was a powerful experience of opening the heart for Steere. Such opening of the heart, as the authors of *Listening Hearts* explain, has meaning beyond its organic functioning: "The title [*Listening Hearts*] rises from the Hebrew-Christian tradition that understands the heart to have more than a physical nature, that sees the heart as the core of the person, at the center of the body, touching all of the body, mind, soul and spirit" (Farnham, et al., 2011, p. 2). They say a listening heart draws us into communion with God. Not surprisingly, listening is the key activity in both Theory U and Quaker discernment. It shapes the first movement of going down the U in Theory U. In Quaker discernment it is a prerequisite to connecting to source – opening to and resting in the Light – then waiting for inner knowing to emerge, although it would not be expressed in this language.

This chapter focuses on opening the mind, heart and will primarily in individual discernment (the next chapter considers opening, particularly of the will, in communal discernment). I explore this by weaving and cross-fertilising practices of listening in Theory U and Quaker discernment – *mutual irradiation* – and seeing where one enriches and extends the other – *complementarity*.

Weaving Theory U and Quaker discernment

Listening is the means to opening mind, heart and will. In Theory U it is the primary tool in the movement down the U and enables connection with Source and inner knowing. For Quakers it is a rich dimension of listening for the movement of Spirit and helps generate the deep interiority of Quaker discernment – seeking "where words come from" and the "experience of confronting the One who listens" (Steere D. V., 1955, p. 17). The two approaches complement and enrich each other and I liken it to weaving. I present listening in Theory U as a vertical warp which gives a structural pattern to a practice of listening; I present Quaker accounts as a horizontal weft that textures and integrates the fabric of discernment. What I hope to show is how each different approach adds resilience and depth to the other.

An overview of listening

Listening is central in Theory U: "The foundational capacity of the U is listening. Listening to others. Listening to oneself. And listening to what emerges from the collective. Effective listening requires the creation of open space in which others can contribute to the whole" (Presencing Institute). Theory U describes four levels of listening (see diagram 10), each related to an aspect of opening. Theory U recognises that the transition from one level to the next may stimulate our resistance and identifies this as three Voices: Judgement (as the mind opens), Cynicism (as the heart opens) and Fear (as the will opens) and each is outlined in my account.

In Theory U successively deeper listening brings the discerner closer and closer to Source and activates a capacity to act from inner knowing. Each level of listening enables a further shift into open mind, open heart and open will. Whilst the levels of listening are necessarily presented as sequential, in reality there will be a lot of crossover between them. They might be likened to a structured working out of what Quakers encompass in the phrase 'coming with heart and mind prepared'. This is extended further, for instance, by Loring's emphasis on listening as the key that unlocks discernment; as quoted earlier she understands listening as far more than auditory listening: "This kind of listening is not simply auditory. It may be visual, kinesthetic, intuitive or visceral as well, depending on the deepest attentiveness natural to the individual" (Loring, 1997, p. 2); this is listening with both breadth and depth. The following passage amplifies how this kind of multi-dimensional listening is experienced in Quaker work in conflict resolution:

"The second skill is the skill of *listening*: listening not just to the words, but to the feelings and needs behind the words. It takes a great deal of time and energy to listen well. It's a kind of weaving: reflecting back, asking for clarification, asking for time in turn to be listened to, being truly open to what we're hearing (even if it hurts), being open to the possibility that we might ourselves be changed by what we hear" (QFP, 2016 para 20.71).

Diagram 10: Theory U: four levels of listening (Scharmer, 2009)

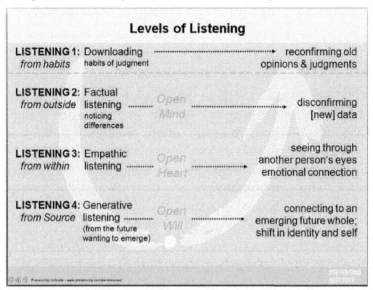

The rest of this chapter describes each of the four levels of listening in Theory U and weaves this alongside tools of discernment drawn from a variety of Quaker and spirit-led sources. They employ listening, in the widest sense indicated by Loring, with warmth combined with rigour and depth. My argument is that together they complement and mutually irradiate the approach each brings.

Warp – listening at level one in Theory U

Downloading is the first level of listening and typifies the start of the journey down the U. It relates to being stuck in old habits. We can confront familiar and unexamined ways of seeing by suspending and setting aside judgements we habitually make. This creates breathing space. I am reminded of the advice by Buddhist nun, Ayya Khema, that when we seek to change our patterns of thinking we should look for some point,

Diagram 11: Level 1 listening

however small, where we can 'loosen at the edges' (Khema, 2002); even a small change will induce further loosening and change. The loosening begins when we begin to pay attention rather than stay on autopilot; paying attention fixes attention on the reality in front of us. Downloading in Theory U denotes unexamined patterns of thinking – assumptions, opinions and judgements – and acts like a closed circle that is stuck in taken-for-granted and unquestioned images of reality. If a positive aspect is added to 'downloading' – gathering and taking stock of what we know so far, gathering factual information and different lines of reasoning – then listening is immediately rounded out to pay attention for valuable material, too.

Theory U notes that we meet our resistance to opening the mind in the Voice of Judgment; in essence this internal voice shuts down our capacity to open to a freer and more creative way of seeing. It leaves us locked in habitual opinions and judgements that protect us from our existential fear that we are not 'safe'. By giving this resistance a name, it highlights an equivalent view in Quaker discernment that frames our personal agendas, interests and habitual patterns as baggage that is to be "left at the door".

Weft – Bieber's three strands of spiritual discernment

Bieber identifies three strands – braids – that weave an active practice of discernment: willingness, attentiveness and responsiveness. The three braids are mutually dependent and interwoven; thus, attentiveness needs our willingness, responsiveness our openness to whatever may come, paying attention to where we are and where Spirit is moving. Listening is a means of noticing the activity and nudges of the Spirit in all three strands.

Bieber sees listening as part of willingness in a similar way to Loring – opening to the light and wisdom of Spirit. She stresses our limitations in making good decisions on our own (Bieber, 2011, pp. 15-45). Bieber describes willingness as a combination of "Help" and "Yes". Willingness says Help as we directly address situations when we fall into familiar opinions and habitual ways of seeing that keep us stuck in that mode of response. When this response is unconscious, we are on autopilot and it is difficult to catch. It is hard to shine a light on our habits even when we are aware we are stuck. After all, that's why they are habitual and feel like a comfort blanket. Willingness adds a subtle lever that sets change in motion. It addresses our fear that we are not safe and challenges our associated desire to make sure we are in control of our lives. Bieber focuses our attention on our resistance as we attempt to release our egoic need for control and engage with God to discover what may be for the best.

Weft – Experiment with Light

Experiment with Light is a Quaker practice based on accounts early Friends gave of their experience. It developed out of the study of the writings of early Quakers by theologian and Quaker Rex Ambler. Experiment with Light is used by small groups meeting together regularly. It is a four-step process rooted in openness to Inward Light and inner knowing. I see it offering something akin to a Quaker methodology of opening mind, heart and will:

- "Mind the Light (pay attention to what's going on inside you, particularly where there's something that makes you feel uncomfortable)

- "Open your heart to the truth (don't run away from anything that's difficult or that you don't want to face, but keep a little distance from it: 'be still and cool in thy mind')

- "Wait in the Light (be patient, let the Light show you what is really going on, ask questions if what is offered to you isn't clear or you want to know more, and wait for the answers to come, don't try to explain)

- "Submit (accept and welcome the information or images, and the insights, dreams and perceptions that may come later, and allow them to show the truth) (Experiment with Light Network, 2015)."

Warp – level two listening in Theory U

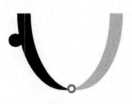

Diagram 12: Level 2- listening

At the second level of listening – factual listening – we listen largely from outside. We notice differences between things and seek to confirm or disprove the facts. This is also a useful part of the Quaker practice of 'coming with heart and mind prepared', but Theory U notes it can be cold and detached. This echoes Bieber explaining detachment as related to fear of change, a defence against new facts that might change one's view. Coldness can be limiting and inhibits opening the mind. But deeper listening requires opening the mind, absorbing a fuller picture of relevant information and facts to give a more rounded picture of the whole. Factual listening must go beyond opinions and points of view. The Quaker practice of coming with heart and mind prepared sets an intention to clarify a matter whilst setting aside personal agendas. In suspending judgement it is helpful to "realise how many troubles arise not from the system, but from our human imperfections and the variety of our temperaments and viewpoints. These meetings are in fact not merely occasions for transacting with proper efficiency the affairs of the church but also opportunities when we can learn to bear and forbear, to practise to one another that love which 'suffereth long and is kind'" (QFP, 2016, para 3.03).

Weft – Bieber's inner gesture and yearning

Bieber addresses opening as an initial inner gesture of simply listening intently to oneself, noticing a yearning for something – however vague – or simply a sense of direction towards some change and now saying 'yes'. She writes: "There is something mysterious about saying 'yes'. It sets things in motion ... In the first minute or two, nothing actually looks different ... We have, however, opened to a specific yet unknown future ... the fact that we've said 'Yes' to it changes things." Bieber continues: "Our 'yes' to God profoundly changes us, too ... We are beginning a specific yet unknown journey into greater harmony with divine music." She quotes Thomas Merton, the Trappist monk: "Our real journey in life is interior; it is a matter of growth, deepening, and of an even greater surrender to the creative action of love and grace in our hearts" (Bieber, 2011, p. 21). Bieber reminds us that the central and first act – what Loring calls "an inner gesture" – is an inner experience of opening to God; she then provides a variety of ways in which we may address our fears – fear of change, of not being in charge, not trusting the guide or that God is not there (Bieber, 2011, pp 21-24).

This illuminates an important distinction between spirit-led discernment and Theory U. In Theory U, the U process culminates in connecting with source and inner knowing. By contrast, Bieber, through her strand of attentiveness, reminds us that our connection with God is listening to that which is present *all* the time. Willingness emphasises consciously opening to God and that which is present. The strand of responsiveness focuses moving into mystery and inviting fluidity and potential. Bieber acknowledges this may feel risky. Sometimes, she says, the heart may be more willing – an open heart – than the mind can yet manage thus the mind resists. Or the mind may be open but the heart feels vulnerable and resists. She sees the body – opening the will – as a way of bringing mind and heart into one. They can be brought into one by responding to the body language of gesture and movement; for example, we bring our hands forward and more expansively when we are willing whereas when we resist our body language is tight and rigid. Thus postures of prayer express acceptance. Consciously adapting our body language stimulates change.

Weft – the Quaker practice of threshing

A Quaker threshing meeting is an extended practice of listening. "Originally the term was used to describe large and noisy meetings for convincement of 'the world's people' in order to 'thresh' them away from the world' (QFP, para 12.26). The purpose is to allow views to be aired in a manner that allows free expression of strong, and potentially controversial, views and conflict without losing sight of a sense of community. This can clear the way for a future meeting to reach a discerned decision. Even if becomes obvious in the threshing that a decision is becoming clear, a separate meeting is called to discern and record the decision. It requires each person and the group as a whole to listen with an open mind and open heart and cultivate deeper opening through non-judgmental listening to a range of views and opinions. Recent research on threshing describes it as a "focus on exploring and understanding the complex, messy and multi-stranded nature of the 'whole of life'. This includes, especially, strong emotions, rational arguments, and disputes about matters of fact – all aspects of our lives that might be set aside or downplayed as a Quaker business meeting reaches a decision, but which need to be heard and taken into account in the preparation for that decision. A threshing meeting is one way in which Quakers can respond *collectively* to the advice to come with heart and mind prepared" (Muers & Grant, 2016, p. 2).

Muers and Grant observe that the aim of threshing – to open both mind and heart to fresh ways of seeing and diverse points of view – is undermined if alternative perspectives are labelled as "the others are doing it wrong". Thus threshing is dependent on individuals recognising resistance surfacing in the form of the Voice of Judgment: attachment, judgement and attitudes that may keep us stuck rather than engaging with an opportunity to "loosen at the edges". Theory U also tells us to pay attention to "cracks" that open, a little incident or remark – even if apparently insignificant – that lets in a different and more inclusive view of a situation enabling the world to open up differently. Such moments are thresholds; the origin of the word threshold is the same as threshing – beating the husks away from the grain. What makes this possible?

The defining element of a threshing meeting is the spirit in which it is held. It upholds the qualitative impact of listening in Quaker meetings: creating a safe space to encourage all to speak; respect even when strong views are expressed; contributions are not made in opposition to each other but as a contribution to the centre of the meeting; care is taken at the time and afterwards for the feelings of those who may be distressed. It helps a group, community or organisation see with fresh eyes as doubts and concern can be voiced without obstructing the eventual decision. It may clear the air and clarify matters, enabling new possibilities to come forward, particularly in the time between the threshing and the decision meeting. Muers and Grant call this culture of a threshing meeting a Quaker 'space'. It facilitates seeing with fresh eyes with care and attention to feeling, a shared desire to reach a discerned decision and a commitment that the eventual decision will be spirit-led. This lays the groundwork for deeper levels of listening as those present access a more open mind and heart. There is an opening of the will as they listen into the spaces between the different points of view and 'hear' where possibilities and potential for the best may emerge.

Warp – level three listening in Theory U

Diagram 13: Level 3 listening

This introduces us to the third level of listening, listening from within. We have a growing sense of wonder as we see there is more beyond the familiar ways of seeing we have inhabited. Now the purpose of listening is to establish an empathic connection with people and with the matter being considered.

To do so we have to break through the Voice of Cynicism that detaches us from wonder, emotion and true connection. Seeing through another person's eyes opens the heart; allowing ourselves to be touched prepares us to see differently too.

Weft – the receptors for listening and attentiveness

Based on readings and interviews with several Friends from Central Philadelphia Monthly Meeting Lee Junker summed up how Quakers approach empathic listening: "One Friend told me that we come not only to listen, but to do so with 'different receptors'. Listening both with head and heart, we try to follow Jesus' admonition to 'stay alert' (Mark 1 3:33). Listening, paying attention and having the intention to do so are critical. Marty Grundy has written: 'Our meetings have a great responsibility to be gatherings of people who are listening to the Inward Teacher, helping each other listen, and learning how to listen together'; Sandra Cronk says: '… it is in worship and business meetings that Friends practice the discipline of listening together'. Pat Loring has written: 'Discernment in this setting is taken in its widest sense of the listening that distinguishes the work of that of God in us from the work of all the other things we carry in us as well.' In order to listen well, we need to leave ample space and silence between speakers and to bring ourselves back into prayer as need arises" (Junker, 2005, p. 7).

This is illustrated in Bieber's third strand of attentiveness (Bieber, 2011, pp. 49-79). She explains attentiveness as coming to see ourselves more clearly as well as paying attention to signals that inform us about our inner journey of discernment. Bieber asserts that what is true and real lies at the heart of spiritual decision-making. Unless we engage with our dreams and yearnings we do not bring them into the light of divine wisdom. As she sees it, attentiveness to diverse ways of knowing simplifies the contradictions and complications in our lives and clarifies finely graded hard choices – those that are not black and white but all shades of grey. In one sense attentiveness focuses on getting to know ourselves more closely and learning our language of communication with God. This asks us to slow down, breathe, pause, be awake, reclaim our sense of wonder and curiosity and give time to practices that bring us closer to this field of energy or quiet, still clarity in ourselves. Bieber guides us in developing attentiveness through learning the language in which the divine speaks: listening to the inner self through heart and mind, dreams and visions, the body and passion; and paying attention to God's nudges. It seems to me this fills out a kind of 'nourishing discernment' that does not hide from the challenges but addresses them in a way that brings some softness and abundance to discernment and prepares us for the next step.

Warp – level four listening in Theory U

Diagram 14: Level 4 listening

The fourth level of listening is associated with the journey across the bottom of the U through to crystallising our discernment. It is the phase when we shift toward seeing the whole, engaging with a field of relationship rather than seeing things only as parts. The boundaries between us, as separate individuals, and the field melt; we experience ourselves as part of the whole. Scharmer quotes cognitive psychologist, Eleanor Rosch, in explaining the term 'field': "In a field, intention, body, and mind become integrated together. You start to be aware of perception happening from the whole field, not from within a separate perceiver ... The heart in any contemplative tradition is not a sentimentality or an emotionality but a deep yogic centerpoint. Opening the heart means accessing and activating the deeper levels of our emotional perception. Listening with the heart literally means using the heart and our capacity for appreciation and love as an organ of perception. At this point, we can actually see with the heart" (Scharmer, 2009, Kindle Loc 2339). Our resistance arises as the Voice of Fear in the face of our vulnerability and trepidation of surrender to God.

Bieber uses a striking metaphor akin to Lonsdale's metaphor of dance: "When we engage in deepened listening, what we are really listening for is the music of the Creator so we can live in better harmony with that music, so we can live within that music" (Bieber, 2011, pp. 82-83).

Weft – responsiveness and being gathered

As we engage with the movement across the bottom of the U, we respond to an impulse to connect to source. Responsiveness is about gaining clarity and acting — or becoming clear it's a time to wait. Responsiveness engages us with the whole, the fourth level of generative listening that is active throughout our listening and waiting, and then crystallising and clarifying the discernment. In Theory U, this goes hand in hand with opening the will and requires slowing down and 'letting go' to lead us into deeper connection. Bieber argues that responsiveness is the movement that helps us articulate our discernment and test it. We learn to intuitively trust step-by-step engagement with guidance – inner listening – in times of waiting and times of activity. She describes it as "the process of creating with God … continually renew[ing] our willing openness to the Light and the landscape within and around us" (Bieber, 2011, p. 7). It is how we stay alert to testing, validating and checking the wisdom we receive. In an apt analogy Bieber likens responsiveness to a complex experiment: she likens our insight, direction or guidance to a 'hypothesis'; we gather evidence to appraise its feasibility; and test it by putting it into practice then evaluate the results and, if necessary, re-calibrate the hypothesis.

Scharmer describes this stage as preparing for deep gathering, sinking to the inner knowing of the heart. This resonates with the Quaker description of 'gathered' for a worshipping group reaching a place of unity with each other and with Spirit:

"A 'gathered' Quaker meeting is something more than a number of individuals sitting down together but meditating individually. So long as each sits in meditation in the way one does when worshipping by oneself, the worship will seldom reach that greater depth which a Quaker meeting at its best achieves. The goal of a truly 'gathered' meeting is to become fused into something bigger than the sum of the parts …

"As a meeting 'gathers', as each individual 'centres down', there gradually develops a feeling of belonging to a group who are together seeking a sense of the Presence. The 'I' in us begins to feel like 'we'. At some point – it may be early in the meeting or it may be later, or it may never occur at all – we suddenly feel a sense of unity, a sense of togetherness with one another and with that something outside ourselves that we call God" (QFP, 2016, para 2.47).

Weft – Liebert: grounding discernment in practices to integrate decisions into the life of faith

I turn lastly to review cross-fertilisation between Theory U and spirit-led discernment as described by Liebert. Liebert presents a range of ways of knowing together with practices for cultivating practical use in a secure and grounded manner. She discusses multiple ways in which God may be at work and in communication in our personal life. Her books draw on Ignatian-based discernment to open up ways of knowing in "seeking God's call in the midst of the decisions that mark one's life" (Liebert, 2008, p. ix). She details a wide range of ways of knowing and practices to develop a personal way of discernment, which is extended in her second book (Liebert, 2015) on discernment in communities and institutions.

For Liebert, the starting point focuses on noticing where God is active in daily life, in mundane as well as significant moments and turning points. We learn to recognise this through a daily practice of Examen, reviewing where God, love, and leading have been active in our life together with knowing ourselves sufficiently to discern the voice of God from all other voices. Another concept is 'spiritual freedom', which Liebert explains as "the inner disposition upon which discernment rests and which creates the climate for discernment" (Liebert, 2008, p. 19). Freedom comes from letting go of the agendas of the world and becoming indifferent to the outcome. She says this lifts discernment beyond self-improvement because we put seeking and responding to God's call first. Liebert says the purpose of discernment is not making a decision but becoming more sensitive and responsive to God's call – as indeed Quakers say listening together to God, not the decision, is the heart of listening spirituality.

The heart of Liebert's book, however, is how she helps the reader "begin to become a discerning person" in a step-by-step progression. This contrasts with the three movements at the heart of a U map as Liebert presents her steps as a list.

- Seek spiritual freedom
- Discover and name the issue or choice you face
- Gather and evaluate appropriate data about the issue

- Reflect and pray

- Formulate a tentative decision

- Seek confirmation

- Assess the process

For Liebert, the essence of the issue and the questions it involves, need to be identified clearly. They also need to be sufficiently concrete for us to work with in our imagination, and this takes constant and persistent listening. The presenting issue may not be the real question and that becomes clear in discussion or as information comes to light. The issue needs to be framed so it is focused yet still held flexibly. The process is dynamic and discernment unfolds organically. Liebert observes that framing the question requires sifting and sorting: "You will likely find that some practices are more sympathetic to the way you naturally process information. I encourage you to notice your preference for certain practices and build them into your personal discernment repertoire. At the same time, be aware that no single process provides a sufficiently complex means of uncovering all that you might need or want to know as you seek God's preferred future" (Liebert, 2008, p. xvii). Wise discernment balances different practices that keep us focused on the realistic possibilities of a situation. She outlines a range of entry points to discernment including memory, intuition, body, imagination, reason, a set of feelings that she calls "religious affections", and nature. This range of entry points are a real strength of her work. She argues that people rely on a wide variety of strategies and techniques, sometimes from personal aptitude, sometimes suggested by the situation: "Some make lists and quite literally think their way to a logical decision. Others recognize a decision in their bodies; they might say, 'I know in my gut this is the right thing to do'. Others come to clarity by taking a long afternoon out in nature, sitting by the ocean or hiking in the hills" (Liebert, 2008, p. xii).

Liebert's book fleshes out the outline map of the U with the detail and understanding she has of the underlying dynamic at work. Her approach to spirit-led discernment and list of alternative approaches, though not exhaustive, helps balance personality and preference in a holistic process in which one practice enhances other approaches.

Reflections: mutual irradiation and complementarity

- Loring's multi-dimensional description of listening makes clear that, at its best, it is a holistic activity. Ultimately, as Steere puts it, authentic acceptance of another – "the listener's capacity to care, to care enough to be involved" – enables you to "listen another's soul in to a condition of disclosure and discovery … in penetrating to what is involved in listening do we not disclose the thinness of the filament that separates men listening openly to one another, and that of God intently listening to each soul?" (Steere D. V., 1955, p. 14) In Theory U Scharmer writes: "When connecting to other people and contexts, activate and open up all four 'channels' of listening: listen from what you know (Listening 1), from what surprises you (Listening 2), from empathizing with the interviewee (Listening 3) and from the deepest source (Listening 4)." He observes that of all the interviewers he has met, Jaworski stands out for his ability to create a trusting connection with the interviewee. When he asked Jaworski about this, Jaworski told him that the most important hour is the one before the interview starts when "he centers himself to open his mind and his heart to the interview about to take place" (Scharmer, 2009, pp. 5870/922, Kindle) – an observation that sums up the nature of all listening for connection and inner knowing.

- Despite the contrasting language and mode of approach between Theory U and spirit-led and Quaker discernment, I find a complementarity that mutually irradiates both. My interweaving between Theory U levels of listening and different Quaker and spirit-led accounts of a listening spirituality attest, I hope, to the complementary strengths of the different sets of practice.

- Theory U has developed a detailed explanation of listening, which supplements, and is supplemented by, Loring's emphasis on discernment as deep listening to God. Between 2010 and 2013, at a time when I was their clerk, the trustees of Quaker Social Action (QSA) carried out an appreciative inquiry into the meaning of the charity's Quaker identity today. Our report stressed the importance of listening to others, to oneself, to the sense of the meeting, and to the movement of spirit in Quaker practice. The trustees confirmed that: "From the very beginnings, the central authority in the embryonic Quaker way was a collective or corporate experience: early Quakers experienced and understood God as accessible to each person – 'listening' to the still small voice and 'hearing' leadings or promptings that gave insight into how to live and how to act. Early Quakers developed ways of listening to such leadings and promptings when they were gathered together – corporate guidance – testing their validity – Truth. This is as important and central to Quakers today as it was in the late seventeenth century, even if the language in which it is expressed reflects more diverse understandings of God" (QSA, 2013, p. 26).

- Theory U is a complex body of material. Therefore, I find the simplicity of a few Quaker phrases, such as coming with heart and mind prepared, helpful. Listening is recognised as a central part of all Quaker practice; this is demonstrated in Loring's books which draw on Quaker and other sources for a variety of modes and forms of listening. However, Quaker prompting to 'listen' is less elaborated. Theory U sets out a progression to ever-deepening levels in connecting to source. Theory U analyses the internal voices that can obstruct our capacity to listen, and this is useful. In the latest developments in his work, Scharmer ties the levels of listening to a model of large scale social and systemic change (Scharmer, 2013).

- Listening in Quaker discernment is more thorough-going in a different way since it comes to a focus around listening to the movement of Spirit, listening to God, listening to the most profound place of creative potential. The writers I draw on in exploring spirit-led and Quaker discernment, principally Loring, Bieber and Liebert, bring resilience and wise softening to the levels of listening in Theory U.

- In summary, therefore, I find the way Theory U organises and explains deepening levels of listening complementary to the listening practices described by writers and in spirit-led discernment practices. They all offer something different. Theory U is a map and route through a single discernment cycle; it identifies steps that need to be accomplished at each level and some associated barriers to progress. Loring, by contrast, brings together a wide range of spiritual practices from many traditions that offer different ways to discern. Bieber, with the simple device of an image of three interweaving strands, presents perhaps the most vivid and clear structure with activities that comprise a thorough and varied approach to discernment. Liebert illustrates an inclusive model drawing strongly on the Ignatian tradition with a broad understanding of the many ways in which we listen and hear in discernment. Other Quaker practices, such as Experiment with Light and threshing, bring life and vitality to the structured levels of listening. I have found that approaches drawn from Theory U and spirit-led discernment mutually irradiate each other.

Chapter 5. Going Round the Bend – Opening the Will

So far my enquiry has reviewed the first, and most substantial, of three movements – going down the left-hand side of the U in a process of opening and deepening. This chapter focuses specifically on the point where, visually, the shape curves toward the bottom of the U. In the initial U diagram, it's a transition toward 'retreat and reflect' and opening the will to inner knowing and guidance arising in the presence of a deep connection with source.

Having concentrated so far on individual discernment, I now return to Benefiel's three-fold model of discernment and consider individual discernment in community and corporate discernment. I explore clearness as an example of individual discernment in community and Quaker business method as an example of collective decision-making. I shall also explore Quaker business method as an example of opening the will to encounter a deep connection with source.

Opening the will – sensing and letting go

As Arthur's three movements developed into Theory U, Scharmer identified the journey down the U as predominantly *sensing*: "When moving from seeing to sensing, perception begins to happen *from the whole field*" (Scharmer O., Theory U, 2009, pp. 2257/9228, Kindle). And again "Almost always, when such a deeper field shift happens, we observe a little previous incident that creates the crack or opening for such a deeper shift. That little spark is often connected with a moment of deep silence and / or a question that comes straight from the heart" (Scharmer, 2009, Loc 2339/9228, Kindle).

This fits with stepping across a threshold and letting go, which prepares us for what Quakers call 'letting in' – opening the will to let Spirit in. Steere describes this experience powerfully in the context of individual discernment: "Have you ever sat with a friend when in the course of an easy and pleasant conversation the talk took a new turn and you both listened avidly to the other and to something that was emerging in your visit? You found yourselves saying things that astonished you and finally you stopped talking and there was an immense naturalness about the long silent pause that followed. In that silent interval you were possessed by what you had discovered together. If this has happened to you, you know that when you come up out of such an experience, there is a memory of rapture and a feeling in the heart of having touched holy ground" (Steere D. V., 1955, p. 1).

This mutuality is particularly evident when people are working together, whether in small groups or larger organisations – wherever they are in community. They begin to talk together and experience their conversation increasingly as if their thinking is in sync; time seems to slow down and the way people relate to each other changes: "Something had moved them beyond their usual state where people argue as separate individuals, as captives inside their own brains" (Scharmer O. 2009, pp. Loc 2294/9228, Kindle). This shift is a significant transition and is experienced particularly powerfully when a group shifts into operating as a whole field and discerns a decision that feels as if it comes from somewhere else altogether. Those Quakers present at the Yearly Meeting Gathering in York in 2009 experienced this in the discussion and discerning of a decision to call for legislation to authorise same sex marriage. Bache wrote about his experience in university teaching that lead him to actively co-operate with fields and collective consciousness with his students. He identifies a step from judging "what someone else says in terms of how compatible it is with our own convictions" to "sometimes we manage to listen from the other person's reference point as when we try to see the world through their eyes". He observed listening together for patterns, insights, and deeper questions. He describes "listening for the middle" or "listening with the third ear" when "one is trying to listen free of self-reference, free of ego". He makes an observation that pinpoints a shift when perception begins to happen from the whole field: "The task is to listen to the whole conversation in order to recognize the larger patterns emerging in it ... one tries to hear the voice of the conversation rather than the voices of its individual members ... it sometimes blossoms into other forms of expansive awareness" (Bache, 2008, pp. 129-131).

Visually on a U map this comes where the shape bends toward connecting to source and listening to inner knowing; kinaesthetically it is as if the body – the organ of implementing the will – sets itself to head in that direction. It is a key moment in a discernment process, opening a heart-centred space as a gateway: "If nobody gets in the way with their own agendas, then we see more possibilities. Once we get over the threshold, there's a certain richness – a collective listening capacity that is humbling" (Scharmer, 2009, Loc. 2252-2444/9228, Kindle). This heart-centred gateway is both horizontal – relationship with each other – and vertical – the heart perceived as the organ of wisdom enabling a group to discern and act from an inner knowing.

However the transition entails going through the eye of the needle – metaphorically squeezing through a narrow entrance and *opening the will* to let go so we can let come from a deeper place; Quakers sometimes speak of "let go, let God". Spiritual discernment as a process draws on the whole self, soul, spirit, mind, heart and body as it deepens into connection with source. Squeezing through this narrow entrance requires us to let go of anything unnecessary, whether fixed ideas and agendas, personal preferences, material attachments or internal resistance. In her work on soul and leadership in organisations, Benefiel describes discernment as a dance of spirituality as "the human spirit, fully engaged" (Benefiel, 2005, p. 9). The rest of this chapter explores this dance, the demands made of the individual to pass through the narrow gate of communal discernment and its relationship to opening the will.

Individual and collective discernment in a group

Some years ago I chaired a writing team collaborating on a book on contemporary spirituality. My lead colleagues, Janice Dolley and Ike Isaksen, and I gathered people whose spirituality was important in their life yet brought different perspectives, most of whom knew each other to some degree. Initially, we spent time sharing our spiritual journeys in threes, noting each person's threads and insights, and assembled this material into a large map of the spiritual journey that shaped the content of the book. The outline of each chapter was agreed and the writers went away each with a chapter to write. Once their drafts were written, these were sent to critical readers who sent their feedback before the team met to review its work and critical readers' feedback. At this point, everything we had written was taken apart as we challenged and critiqued each other's work. Then we reflected together in stillness, using the ways of noticing described earlier, listening for a way forward, until someone would share an insight that enabled us to co-design the next round of writing and we went through the cycle again. We faced a challenging decision over how to present our collaboration. Some wanted each chapter written entirely by one person so the chapters expressed different voices in contemporary spirituality. Some preferred each chapter to be developed successively by different writers. We discussed and reflected and discerned that we would express our voices as one.

We worked in all three dimensions of Benefiel's model of discernment; we discerned as individuals, we discerned in smaller groups at the meetings and we discerned collectively as we sought insight as a collaborative team. It represented a real squeezing through a narrow gate, opening the will of every team member so the team could function as one, drawing on a shared inner knowing to guide our work. As I reflect on this experience now, I see it as resonant with my Quaker experience of a discernment process and the U describes the journey we undertook with our writing.

Each team member discerned individually as they reflected on their own spiritual journey and each piece of writing emerged out of the discernment of the person writing that chapter (discerning that of God in themselves and their experience). As individuals, we brought our material to each other; the writing group became a community where we could share issues, difficulties and questions thus the material was threshed. The group reviewed everything together, addressed thorny issues and sometimes clarifying them in a manner similar to clearness. We waited together until we saw how to proceed by letting in inner knowing in a corporate discernment. We refined what was to be done and by whom (sense of the meeting), pondering on it until we were content (we clerked our agreement). Everyone went away and wrote according to this plan (prototyping) until, following the second cycle, it was agreed I would complete a final edit and preparation for publication (performing). The entire writing took eight months (act swiftly) (Dawes, et al., 2005). Our work depended on deep and open listening to each other and each writer opening their will and squeezing through the eye of the needle. The hardest decision was deciding to blend our personal authorship into one (reach unity). It is hard as a writer to surrender and let go of all the ideas and phrases you have laboured over so another person can discern what to keep or discard of your work. The process that squeezed us through this narrow gate was made possible by opening our minds to the diverse material we worked on, opening our hearts to write together, and opening our personal and collective will to a task we felt called to take on. We sought to make each decision for the best in the hope the book would be useful for others.

All these elements can be observed, and more, in both Theory U and Quaker discernment processes such as clearness and Quaker business method.

Individual discernment in community – clearness

Clearness is a distinctive Quaker contribution to spirit-led discernment. The purpose of clearness is to offer an individual (focus person) the support of a group in wrestling with a decision or question; the example above showed clearness being used to help a focus person – the writer – consider thorny issues in their writing. Clearness is not about giving the focus person advice, resolving conflicts or solving problems but rather "By focusing on a particular issue, a meeting for clearness enables everyone present to become 'clear' about possible options and ways forward" (QFP, 2016, para 12.24). Early Quakers began to ask "am I / are we clear?" as a check on nagging questions, doubts, uncertainties – 'stops' – in the mind of someone discerning their way forward. Spiritually, clearness rests on the belief that: "Each of us has an inner teacher, a voice of truth, that offers the guidance and power we need to deal with our problems. But that inner voice is often garbled by various kinds of inward and outward interference. The function of the Clearness Committee is not to give advice or 'fix' people from the outside in but rather to help people remove the interference so that they can discover their own wisdom from the inside out" (Palmer, 2009, p. 1).

A clearness process is held in a structured and timed spirit of Quaker worship and depends on listening, trust and respect. From the perspective of Theory U, it epitomises listening with the whole person and listening to the whole field. Such listening is not simply the group listening to the focus person outline the issue brought to clearness. It is inner listening, listening with the third ear, with all present seeking inner knowing. This upholds the inner knowing of the focus person and the inner listening of the group. It enables the focus person's inner knowing beyond what Palmer calls 'internal noise' and interference. Palmer, an American Quaker, is particularly associated with reviving the use of clearness. Whilst Palmer encourages a clearness process of up to two hours, Benefiel often uses mini-clearness in a tightly timed and structured process with a focus person, between two and five or six people and the mini-clearness cycle taking twenty to thirty minutes. A clearness process is confidential and the insights, questions, observations or images offered used or discarded wholly at the discretion of the focus person as they discern their inner knowing. Initially, many people find it difficult to conduct clearness as it reveals our tendencies to behave as if we know what is best for someone else, whereas clearness is solely about the focus person accessing their own inner knowing.

Well-conducted clearness, with clear guidelines and structure, is a powerful practice. I am one of a three who meet for spiritual friendship; we use this kind of structure informally and find it works well as we value the insight, questions and listening we give and receive in turn. The discipline and protocols of clearness are critical; conducted without that spirit and discipline, it can be hurtful and damaging. Palmer writes: "It is not for extremely fragile people or for extremely delicate problems. But for the right person, with the right issue, it is a powerful way to rally the strength of community around a struggling soul, to draw deeply from the wisdom within all of us. It teaches us to abandon the pretence that we know what is best for another person and instead to ask those honest and open questions that can help that person find his or her own answers. It teaches us to give up the arrogant assumption that we are obliged to 'save' each other and learn, through simple listening, to create the conditions that allow a person to find his or her wholeness within" (Palmer, 2009, p. 4).

This kind of individual discernment in community calls for letting go on the part of both the focus person and the clearness group. For the focus person, letting go requires they set aside preconceived notions of their way forward to be open to inner knowing. For the clearness group, letting go requires them to release ideas they may hold about the issue brought for clearness. Corporate discernment broadens the exercise of letting go as each member of the community makes a journey through the eye of the needle.

Corporate discernment

Discernment in community – corporate discernment – is practised by many groups, secular and spirit-led. The examples in my enquiry are Theory U as a secular model rooted in inner knowing, and spirit-led models from Quaker and, to a lesser degree, Ignatian practice; they are illustrative rather than definitive examples. My purpose is not describing Quaker business method in detail but to consider the discernment process in relation to a U map and the associated inner journey.

Stephenson says that corporate discernment is most effective when done in community: "The great religious teachers realised that discernment is more effective when done in community, so the Buddha, Jesus, Muhammad, and George Fox gathered groups of people who thought along similar lines to themselves. It can be hard when we find cherished opinions being challenged, but community imposes an extra layer of discipline on our wayward, headstrong sense of self, and makes it more likely that any true discernments we have will survive" (Stephenson, 2013).

Sweeney sees corporate discernment as a forum in which "contemplative dialogue creates a liminal space for the deep listening from which communal discernment emerges" and "When we approach communal discernment through this medium of contemplative dialogue, our way of being together becomes a religious experience enacted in community, a communal experience of God 'in whom we live and move and have our being' (Acts 17:28) that draws forth from within us creative intelligence and wisdom." She explains: "The word dialogue comes from two Greek words — *dia* which means 'through' and *logos* which refers to 'meaning' — that invite us into a way of thinking, speaking, and listening with others so that we participate in a flow of shared meaning. Contemplative dialogue, deeply grounded in silence, allows us to experience a profound state of shared consciousness as we listen from the fullness of who we are, speak to one another with humility, candor, trust, and vulnerability, and open ourselves to being transformed by what we hear" (Sweeney, 2014).

In coming to corporate discernment each individual has to bring all of themselves to being discerning whilst letting go of any personal agenda, reactive judgements and 'baggage' in order to let in awareness of the movement of Spirit. In the language of Theory U, clear corporate discernment depends upon generative listening. The intention is that such deep listening generates a shared consciousness or space in which those present think as one organic whole – a corporately discerning field. Initially, we might expect to observe those present saying and thinking the same thing. But, according to the Ignatian tradition, corporate discernment manifests as the Holy Spirit works in and through each actively discerning individual. Through numerous rounds of reflection these individual discernments align into a single view to which there are no longer what Quakers would call 'stops'; this is recognised as the inner knowing of the group. Sweeney links this communal inner knowing to Teilhard de Chardin's idea of the 'noosphere'; the noosphere is perceived as the thinking layer of planet Earth, a sphere of thought encircling the earth, embracing both thought and consciousness. Others equate it to putting on the mind of Christ – being called into unity with a loving Spirit.

The inner journey of corporate discernment

I said earlier the U map is a gateway to the inner journey of discernment and this is the aspect of spirit-led discernment to which I turn. I see the inner journey of discernment nurtured by a process that enables the group to discern the movement of Spirit. This process generates a 'container' that can hold – contain – the group and its work as it discerns the movement of Spirit. The container needs to provide for: the structure of the process – which might be likened to a map or set of guidelines; the culture of decision-making, the norms, values and behaviours; and rituals or practices which enable a community to reach the depth of connection they need for authentic discernment. American Quaker Bill Taber, noting the transformation that can happen in a gathered Meeting for Worship, observed: "Meeting for worship is a Quaker technology for shifting levels of consciousness" (Martin, 2016).

Quaker business method is a Quaker Meeting for Worship called to attend to the business and administrative responsibilities of the worshipping community. My account draws primarily, but not solely, on Quaker business meeting and includes recent observations by participants on a course on discernment who wanted to extract the essentials of discernment to take it into other meetings they attend. This transfer of experience is pertinent to Quaker-led charities and organisations currently grappling with welcoming their first non-Quaker members to a governing board thus inducting non-Quakers into Quaker business method.

Structure

I start with a description of discernment in community by Morris and Olsen (CTUCC, 2014). Between them, the two authors combine experience of a wide range of methods of discernment – Presbyterian, Methodist, Roman Catholic Ignatian, Benedictine and Quaker discernment. Their ten spiritual discernment movements (named in italics) aim to help church communities make decisions. The sequence of movements echo processes we have met already. *Framing* articulates the question so it is identified and clearly stated. *Grounding* anchors discussion in principles or values that will guide discernment. *Shedding* is an invitation to lay aside ego, preconceived notions, false assumptions, biases, and any pre-determined conclusions so the discerning group can fully consider the matter. In *rooting*, the church community draws on Biblical stories, themes and images that relate to the matter to be considered and their faith 'story' before *listening* to God, to each other and to the voices of other stakeholders affected by any decision made. The community then uses imagination and creativity in *exploring* possible options consistent with the key principles and values already identified. The principle 'for the best' is active as they pray and work in *improving* at least three of the most promising options until each is as best they can imagine in line with God's call. In *weighing*, the options are assessed in response to the leading of God's spirit before *closing* on one that is selected. Finally the community "tests the decision by *resting* the discernment near the heart to determine whether it brings primarily feelings of consolation (a sense of peace and movement toward God) or desolation (distress and movement away from God)" (CTUCC, 2014).

Morris and Olsen's ten movements embody good meeting practice and a generic process for opening the mind through sifting and challenging existing information and exploring new options. It gives space to address feelings, pain, hurt and misunderstanding with compassion. The steps call on the discerning group to put aside ego to hear from a wide range of people who may be affected both within and beyond the discerning group; this is an act of opening the heart. The group invites inner knowing in bringing imagination and creativity to reflecting on the options. The central point remains discernment for the best, articulated in this context as the leading of God's spirit.

Culture

Here my source is the report *The Q-bit* compiled by the trustees of Quaker Social Action. A significant part of the QSA inquiry was spent on a detailed exploration of Quaker business method, and sharing this with other Quaker-led organisations and groups to distil the qualities, attributes and behaviours that underpin this practice.

Trust is at the heart of Quaker business method, demonstrated by integrity in external relationships and respect between the people involved. In spirit-led discernment trust is also experienced at a deeper level; it is as if the shared interiority of the discernment process generates an inner-side to trust as well.

QSA trustees reported: "The inner-side of trusteeship gives life and vitality to the cherished values and purposes of an enterprise and the unfolding of its creative founding spirit – what Otto Scharmer describes as 'the deeper source, the inner place from which an individual or a system operates'." The trustees continued: "It is subtle to discern and elusive to articulate, but arguably needs to be explored and renewed once in every generation if an organisation is to be vibrant and robust in fulfilling its purpose whilst resilient and flexible in meeting change. This has added power when the inner-side of trusteeship is rooted in the lived experience of a spiritual and religious community, bears fruit in its values, ways and practices and is expressed in its governance, ways of working and the impact of its work in the world.

"This trusteeship, as Quakers experience it, is fundamentally founded on *trust*:

- Trust in the discoveries of the spiritual practices of early Quakers

- Trust in the process and discipline of Quaker business methods

- Trust in the differing perceptions and experience of Spirit within a group of Quakers

- Trust that – if we listen deeply to the promptings of love and truth – the decisions we make are spirit-led

- Trust that we can learn how to discern and test their validity

- And trusting what Quakers call 'that of God' in each and every person" (QSA, 2013, p. 9).

QSA trustees focused a session of their appreciative inquiry on the nuts and bolts of Quaker business method, noting what was happening when it was used skilfully and when it was under strain. This helped them better understand how trust is established. Quaker business method is a whole; whilst its parts can be examined in their own right, it has to be experienced and cultivated as a whole. Moreover, it is a whole which develops a flow and a generative energy. Eccles summed this up saying: "It is our experience that group decision making is an act of corporate worship, a time when we come together to open our hearts to God's leadings in ourselves and in others. Although this is often referred to as seeking 'the will of God' I prefer to think of decision making as a creative process ... What matters is not so much the decision as the process, a process of the corporate discovery of a way forward which is true to our experience of God's world" (Eccles, 2000). QSA trustees distilled the essence of the culture of Quaker business method in the chart below from their report; the detail can be found by reference to their complete report.

Diagram 15: Key elements in Quaker business methods

- **Building and maintaining trust** – in each other, in the process and in robust reflection on issue
- **Clear and mindful processes**
- The unique Quaker practice **of writing a minute of discussion and decision contemporaneously** in a meeting as part of **a mindful search for unity** and **shared ownership of decisions**
- **Silence and inward reflection** to start meetings and return to periodically **during the flow of the business**
- A non-hierarchical perspective **open to wisdom wherever it arises**
- **Shared values**
- **Allowing the way forward to open through deep listening** rather than be imposed by a timeframe or agenda
- Holding a long-term view that is **willing to act 'outside the box'**
- **Giving matters the time they need**, whether that is a difficult decision, staff giving attention to service users, or trustees **waiting for clearness** in discerning actions Trying always to remain open to '**the flow of a larger intelligence**'
- Trying always to remain **open to 'the flow of a larger intelligence'**

The manner in which spirit-led discernment is upheld is vital. A final extract from the QSA report illustrates some essential conditions that, in the Quaker model, constitute what is called 'Quaker discipline'. These include: frequent use of, thus comfort with, silence; deep listening to others, to oneself, to the sense of the meeting, to the direction of spirit; shared responsibility; speaking to the centre in a meeting not in dialogue with each other; plain speaking; hearing the 'measure of the Light' in all views and voices; respect; coming with heart and mind prepared and open; non-hierarchical and non-judgmental attitudes; holding on to the big picture; seeking clarity about the way forward.

The ten spiritual discernment movements set out by Morris and Olsen are reflected in the picture of Quaker business method in the QSA report. They correspond with the opening of mind, heart and will in Theory U, which, in that model, is accomplished through ever-deepening levels of listening. In combination I find they mutually irradiate the account of each community of practice.

Activities

In Theory U, deepening levels of listening are enabled through activities that help the discerner engage with the issue in a way that opens their mind and heart. Similarly, in Morris and Olsen's ten spiritual discernment movements, this is accomplished by finding biblical stories that correspond to the issue in some way and engage with those affected.

A quality at the heart of Quaker business method is a way of listening that has depth – hearing beyond the words – and is active – facilitating opening of, and to, the heart. The opportunity to open mind and heart is part of Quaker discipline. This discipline comprises norms and guidelines that are an integral part of Quaker discernment rather than simply an authoritarian overlay. It is woven into the fabric of the meeting through clear and mindful processes: a fluency that facilitates the flow of the meeting, agenda preparation, consultation, threshing, clearness, discernment leading to taking a decision, contemporaneous minuting, and prompt follow-up to a meeting such as distribution of a minute to those concerned in the matter (QSA, 2013, p. 24-33). The confidence of trusting that these practices will be adhered to frees up each individual to give their attention fully to inward listening, bringing the rational and intuitive mind into one.

The end point is that decisions are made in the light of people knowing each other in that which is eternal; furthermore both those affected and the issue at hand are 'known' in the same manner as they are gathered into the sense of the meeting. In this way the process of Quaker business method acts as a container that enables a group to connect to source and open to its corporate inner knowing – discernment as making decisions for the best.

Reflections: a different way of working

- At a recent course on discernment, participants wanted to distil elements from Quaker discernment they could take into the range of situations and organisations they encounter. They explored this first by considering what we mean by the phrase 'trusting the process' and then taking the phrase to a mini-clearness process. They took the phrase 'trusting the process' to mean the qualities, attitudes and behaviours conducive to an effective meeting and well-grounded discernment and discussed the qualities, attitudes and behaviours they thought were needed in a meeting in order to trust the process that would ensue.

- They compiled a comprehensive list of characteristics for a process to work well: being present; being open-minded; honest and transparent; respectful; disciplined; courageous; prepared; listening spiritually; inclusive; knowing what the process is and experience of using it; follow up; trust; truthfulness; feeling of being heard; focus; heart and mind prepared; making space; putting aside of self; willingness to be surprised; sufficient time; knowing that what we're doing is bigger than us.

- The group then brought a question to the adapted clearness meeting. A person who had posed a question about difficult meetings acted as the voice of the question. In place of clarifying questions to the focus person, other members of the group acted as supplementary voices for the question as the 'issue' took shape. The group initially gathered some ideas in sharing what worked well. They moved into a deeper reflective stillness as they offered words, images and phrases in bringing clearness to their question.

- No new processes, values or behaviours came to light. But there was a deeper confidence and trust in the value of modelling the principles of spirit-led discernment, their own capacity to initiate change by quiet yet clear and discerned action and the need to train others in the culture of a different way of decision-making. They felt more confident that they could explain to others the intention of discernment as making decisions for the best.

- Clearness is a useful process well-deserving its greater use. I have found it useful whether I've been the focus person or in the supporting circle to offer insight. Each clearness, in its own way, constitutes a 'circle of presence' in which participants hold one another in their future highest potential. Clearness is a useful discernment tool in spiritual friendship and group spiritual nurture and learning. The keys are understanding the clearness process and an ability to uphold the structure.

- A clearness process itself reflects the general U pattern of going down, connecting to source to allow inner knowing to emerge before going up. A U shape is so ubiquitous that it is unclear whether it is simply a universal shape of a discernment process or such a generalised description that most examples fit into it.

- At the start I identified three distinctly different contexts described as discernment: being discerning; a collective method of decision-making and testing the validity of inner knowing recorded as a decision and testing this through action. Clearness and Quaker business method demonstrate all three discernment modes though slightly differently. Both invite all present into being discerning; both describe a whole process that is based on discernment. Arguably discernment in clearness comes as the individuals in the group offer intuitive insight and again as the focus person utilises their insight as they further discern their inner knowing on the matter brought to clearness. Discernment as a specific stage of Quaker business method involves all present in being discerning throughout the business meeting. It has similarities to Ignatian discernment where the leading of the Holy Spirit emerges and is confirmed by the views of the members of the group coming into alignment. It requires further research to explore whether reaching consensus in this manner is substantively different to reaching unity in a Quaker business meeting.

- The experience I recount of writing a book collaboratively was a notable example of discernment. It was challenging but making decisions for the best is complex. Retrospectively, using Quaker business method as an analytical framework to reflect on the experience helps me understand why, and how, this collaborative writing was such a significant experience for me. Quaker business method can be an analytic and reflective tool as well as a meeting process. After Britain Yearly Meeting a small group meets to review 'the manner of holding' and presumably reflects in this way on the large annual gathering and how effectively the process of Quaker business method was used.

- The way Quaker business method works is not fully evident to those coming new to Quakers. Following the behavioural guidelines, for instance standing to speak and speaking only when invited by the clerk, adheres to the letter of the practice but is not, in itself, assurance of its spirit.

- The Quaker Institute for the Future has experimented with ways of carrying out spirit-led research using adaptations of Quaker business and other practices for making discerned communal decisions (Cox, 2014). Their reports are wise reflection on Quaker discernment and practice, not least, from my point of view, as they also write collaboratively in a group and with an explicit Quaker perspective. They identify five phases in collective decision-making, although they say they are not neatly sequential; they observe, as I have found in exploring Theory U, there is overlap and movement back and forth between the phases of: quieting impulses; addressing concerns; exploring responses and gathering shared insights; finding clearness; and bearing witness. Each phase can be seen as a step and as an integral part of the whole process, present at all times.

- Liebert also considers the congruence between a Social Discernment Cycle and Theory U. She points out that Theory U has gone through numerous iterations, each one highlighting a slightly different aspect of Theory U as a dynamic process flow for change. She picks out an aspect of Theory U I omitted for simplicity as particularly relevant to communal discernment – co-sensing illustrated on the next page.

Diagram 16: The U as One Process with 5 Movements
(Scharmer O. 2007, p. 8)

1. CO-INITIATING: Build Common Intent stop and listen to others and to what life calls you to do

5. CO-EVOLVING: Embody the new in eco-systems that facilitate seeing and acting from the whole

2. CO-SENSING: Observe, Observe, Observe go to the places of most potential and listen with your mind and heart

4. CO-CREATING: Prototype the new in living examples to explore the future by doing

3. PRESENCING: Connect to the Source of Inspiration and Will, go to the place of silence and allow the inner knowing to emerge

Chapter 6. Across the Bottom – The Inner Place From Which We Operate

As our discernment moves across the bottom of the U it reaches the heart of the process. At this point we can see how radical, yet integral, it is to make decisions in the light of connecting with source and listening to inner knowing.

Theory U recognises that this discerning approach to decision-making depends on the inner place from which we operate. This insight arose in an interview that Scharmer did with Bill O'Brien, late CEO of Hanover Insurance, who said: "The success of an intervention depends on *the interior condition* of the intervener." We might say it this way: "the success of our actions ... does not depend on *What* we do or *How* we do it, but on the *Inner Place* from which we operate" (Presencing, 2016). Scharmer later concluded this inner place is in *the blind spot* of our everyday experience, outside the range of our normal observation, attention, and awareness. However, in discernment it is a critical factor, both for the individual and for a group.

It seems to me that if we are to reflect on the inner place from which we each operate, we must question our framework of experience, belief and values. This chapter, therefore, is a reflection on four conditions that affect our own inner place, expressed as questions to stimulate your own reflection.

Firstly, it is a tenet of Quakerism that we can each experience Spirit directly; therefore, can we become more open to the words and framework that, for each individual and community of practice, are a valid reflection of *their* experience of the nature of source and inner knowing? Secondly, I consider what might be implied by making decisions for the best; what is our reference point for the best and for the good of the whole? Thirdly, I outline how Jaworski, one of the authors of *Presence*, understands Source; can the boundary of community contain experience that recognises Source and inner knowing without naming it as God alongside those whose authenticity is rooted in a notion of God? Finally I explore an aspect of the taken-for-granted assumptions of a Western scientific model that put invisible boundaries around the inner place from which we can operate; what do we take to be intelligence and valid ways of knowing?

Inner Knowing

In Theory U decisions express the outcome of connecting to Source and discerning inner knowing. Yet inner knowing – a phrase introduced by Brian Arthur – is little considered or explored. It is occasionally linked to intuition, inner knowing of the heart, more authentic higher aspects of our self, with the individual's highest future potential or the future that wants to emerge. The closest Theory U comes to an explanation derives from presencing, a blended word combining "sensing" (feeling the future possibility) and "presence" (the state of being in the present moment): thus, presencing means "sensing and actualizing one's highest future possibility — acting from the presence of what is wanting to emerge. This is still a vague concept, although it indicates that decisions are made with reference to a non-rational set of assumptions and values. Source is also a vague concept beyond being an inner, and deepest, place in us. Perhaps a key addition that Theory U makes to the idea of discerning for the best is the idea that the quality of what we create in any kind of social system is dependent on our quality of awareness, attention, or consciousness – the inner place from which we operate. This feels more recognisable and can stir us into qualitative inward reflection.

For Quakers, the nature of connection to source and inner knowing is focused on attuning to a source that, from the times of early Friends, is frequently known as God without laying down how the nature of God is defined or understood. It is problematic because God is a term that many find uncomfortable. Hence, our intention is making decisions for the best by reference to a transcendent source, Mystery, Energy, Spirit or higher consciousness, but the idea can only be discussed with difficulty. I suggest that many Quakers might recognise what is meant by "the inner place from which we operate" in terms of our inward life, values and the experience of being prompted by an energy or impulse that springs from somewhere larger than our small self. What is clear is that discernment embraces a considered way of deciding that is resonant with our deepest values and calls forth action guided by wisdom, compassion, love and truth. Some may call this God and others express it in a variety of ways.

78

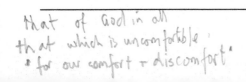

That of God in all
that which is uncomfortable
* for our comfort + discomfort

Each different kind of explanation of source and inner knowing attempts to faithfully express the truth of each community's experience. And each one points to a deeper mystery, and acts as a 'calling card' that invites those to whom it speaks into a deeper relationship. As we reflect on the inner place from which we operate, we must also find how to determine what is for the best and reflect on the nature of the source of inner knowing.

Making decisions for the best

The participants at a discernment course described earlier also considered what 'for the best' meant to them. What did this mean in terms they were comfortable with? A few of their suggestions were:

- What love requires of me / us?

- What can I go forward with comfortably / confidently?

- What would God do / say / suggest here or now?

- Imagine standing in the sense of peace / relief / rightness etc. that comes with a well discerned decision; consider what would help get there

- How do we use heart, mind and body so that our humanness and that of others is kept at the centre?

- What would love say or do here – as softer in tone than 'what would love require'?

'For the best' suggests that relevant facts alone are insufficient to determine a way forward. A choice must be made between alternatives, perhaps involving our priorities, needs, preferences, personal history and vulnerabilities, and our values. Our decisions are so routinely influenced by subjective personal judgement that its influence is unrecognised without effort to make it explicit. Making decisions for the best must, therefore, establish how we assess what is for the best by reference to some kind of measuring rod with the decision weighed and tested in this light. For instance, for many Quakers the measuring rod is seeking the will of God or being spirit-led.

A familiar measuring rod is when a decision is measured against personal conscience or integrity. Another yardstick for evaluating for the best is whether the chosen values of a course of action are universally endorsed. Values such as love, truth, peace, compassion, for example, are embraced by all religious and philosophical traditions. The Golden Rule establishes a maxim of treating others as you wish to be treated yourself. In recent years decisions have come to be weighed against a principle of sustainability and the present and future needs of all life on the planet; a popular example is the Iroquois Nation's reference to the impact of a decision over seven future generations. Deborah Rowlands points out a tension between this and the principle from Theory U to act swiftly to bring the new into being albeit in an experimental prototype that can be adapted. She cautions that "feeling that one has to be sure before proceeding with any change makes everything remarkably cautious, so freeing oneself, and an organisation to say, let's try, this doesn't have to be the same for ever and ever, we can adapt and improve as we go along, seems an important place to be."[9]

The measuring rod may be a revered person. For Christians this will usually be Jesus. Examples of contemporary figures whose standards command worldwide respect are Gandhi, Martin Luther King, Mother Teresa, and Nelson Mandela.

In religious communities, the measuring rod is a spiritual source. Generally, when we think of a transcendent source, the word that comes to mind is God, whether sensed as 'god out there', a voice within or 'that of God'. In other faiths this source may be named, for example, as Allah, Atma, or the Tao. Conventional images of God are increasingly replaced by connection with a deep source in an encounter that may be profound and transformative. What Marion called 'the death of a mythic god' (Marion, 2004) is not death of a sense of the sacred or Spirit but death of the myth of God as a deity in the sky and separate from us. Sweeney writes: "Our image of God has shifted from a Divine Being who intervenes from above and outside us to Spirit's Presence empowering and guiding us and all creation from within" (Sweeney, 2014). Typically, conventional images that liken God to a person give way to something with no figurative qualities – American Quaker Bill Taber, for instance, spoke of "a living, invisible stream of reality" (Taber, 1992, p. 6). Such an invisible stream may be experienced as variably as intuitive insight or a felt-sense of potential or an energy which is experienced as creative and

---

[9] From personal correspondence

intelligent. Scientists report intuitive insight in their process of discovery; Jonas Salk, the inventor of the polio vaccine, spoke of tapping into the continually unfolding 'dynamism' of the universe, and experiencing its evolution as "an active process that ... I can guide by the choices I make" (Loring, 1992, p. 8).

Descriptions of a source or authority offer a narrative that is precious to those for whom it is a faithful expression of their experience and understanding. Gwyn points out: "We interpret where the light is leading us through various frameworks of understanding. ... We understand our 'experience' in part through various interpretive models" (Gwyn, 2014, p. 46). At the same time it is important to recognise that researchers into religious experience such as William James, Alister Hardy and David Hay, tell us that an essential experience of something-more appears in the narratives of virtually all societies.

There appears to be near universal experience of energy that manifests as a life force; humankind is understood as inherently part of this. The life force is present in all life on the planet and the energy sustaining this life force has a consciousness that is beyond our comprehension and experienced as creativity, wisdom, intelligence and love. As humankind we can attune to this energy, connect with its life force, and seek to align our behaviour and action with what we discern as the most fruitful way it can be expressed in the present. To the extent that humankind can open its mind and heart to qualities of creativity, wisdom, intelligence, and love, we can behave and act from increasingly higher levels of human consciousness.

Referring to a source or authority is a call to goodness. But we need to be aware that a call to goodness may be sabotaged, especially when the source of authority is cited as God. At an individual level, simply claiming a decision is discerned as the will of God can unconsciously seek to manipulate a decision whilst allowing human ego to reign unchecked. At the level of groups, organisations and nation states, the havoc and brutality resulting from distorted claims to know the will of God perversely witness to the potency of God as a source of authority. But every distorted claim to be following the will of God contributes to loss of trust in God as a source of spiritual authority. When violent action is labelled as the will of God, people blame God as well as the perpetrators. This highlights the difference between taking a phrase, such as 'following the will of God', literally and understanding it as a metaphor. However God is imaged, following the will of God may be perceived as a metaphor that points toward our interaction with source, a relationship with our deepest inner place; for many this is transcendent (although variously described) whilst for others, as this chapter indicates, this is indeterminate.

In summary, discernment for the best needs to be a considered matter, reflecting a sound basis for decision-making that seeks the wider good. It requires reflection into the source of the guidance or insight and how discernment is grounded in regular reflective practice and validated through testing in action.

Thinking about Source

The experience we each have of our connection to a source differs, whether we perceive it as transcendent in some way or rooted in us. The language, images and concepts we use to talk about the nature of this source expresses what is faithful to our experience and understanding. When we think about the nature of the source from which we act, we may try to make sense of it within our worldview, within current scientific knowledge, within a religious or philosophical tradition we adhere to or some comparable underpinning framework of our belief. Some of us stay with a framework of belief over a lifetime, for some it is more fluid and changeable. We are living in a time when concepts of the nature of God are fluid; this is reflected for example in the difficulty many Quakers have in speaking about the nature of the source from which they act.

Alone of the co-authors of *Presence*, Jaworski made studying Source a focus in his books and papers exploring transformational leadership. He expresses as his central view: "There is a creative Source of infinite potential enfolded in the universe. Connection to this Source leads to the emergence of new realities – discovery, creation, renewal and transformation. We are partners in the unfolding of the universe" (Jaworski, 2012, Loc 66/3302, Kindle) and "Humans can learn to draw from the infinite potential of the Source by choosing to follow a disciplined path toward self-realization and love, the most powerful energy in the universe" (Jaworski, 2012. Loc 57/3302, Kindle).

For Jaworski, Source cannot be fully defined but it can be experienced. He explains: "…there is an underlying intelligence within the universe, which is capable of guiding us and preparing us for the futures we must create" (Jaworski, 2012. Loc 788/3302, Kindle). "We are partners in the evolution of the universe" (Jaworski, 2012. Loc 170/3302, Kindle). By implication, the universe cannot evolve without us and there is a way that individuals and teams or organisations can learn to sense the way the future wants to unfold and enable that unfolding. Jaworski sets down his understanding of the Source in the principles in the box below.

Diagram 17: Jaworski's Four Principles of Source

1. There is an open and emergent quality to the universe.
A group of simple components can suddenly re-emerge at a higher level of self-organization as a new entity with new properties. We can't find a cause or reason for this emergent quality, but as we experience it again and again, we see that the universe offers infinite possibility.

2. The universe is a domain of undivided wholeness; both the material world and consciousness are parts of the same undivided whole.
The totality of existence is enfolded within each fragment of space and time –whether it is a single object, thought, or event. Thus, everything in the universe, including human intentions and ways of being, affects everything else, because everything is part of the same unbroken whole.

3. There is a creative Source of infinite potential enfolded in the universe.
Connection to this Source leads to the emergence of new realities – discovery, creation, renewal, and transformation. We are partners in the unfolding of the universe.

4. Humans can learn to draw from the infinite potential of the Source by choosing to follow a disciplined path toward self-realization and love, the most powerful energy in the universe.
The path may include teachings from ancient traditions developed over thousands of years, contemplative practices, and direct exposure to the generative process of nature.

Although his narrative does not employ 'God language', Jaworski recounts being influenced by a teacher who responded to his question about the difference between Source and God by saying that there's a thin line between them. Throughout Jaworski's explanations of Source are references to love as the force which directs all our actions. At the end of Jaworski's book *Source*, he returns to the teacher who had said there was a thin line between the nature of Source and God. Jaworski makes sense of this by seeing Source as preceding God, more like Tillich's concept of the Ground of Being. It is an impersonal concept whereas God is more personal and, therefore, in some ways easier to relate to. The ultimate reality is so far beyond our comprehension it is equally beyond our concept of God. Jaworski concludes that some theologians prefer Tillich's more abstract term the Ground of Being because it is free of the cultural associations that cling to the word God. If Source and Ground of Being are not so distant from each other conceptually, Jaworski reasons, and if the Ground of Being is compatible with one's idea of God, then the gap between Source and God is indeed thin.

Ways of knowing and intelligence

The inner place from which we operate is heavily dependent on our worldview – our model of reality. One of the steps in Theory U is to set aside taken-for-granted knowing, unrecognised assumptions and habitual ways of thinking. Thus, in conclusion, I speculate about ways of knowing and intelligence, with the intention of being provocative. From my point of view, we cannot know the nature of God, but we can assimilate new knowledge that tells us that there is more to sensing and responding to fields of awareness than we have assumed. The God we know works in more remarkable ways than we thought.

On the first morning of the Eva Koch residential study period, during morning Quaker Meeting for Worship I sat looking at a tree that has stirred my reflections before. I asked myself: *Does a tree discern – make decisions for the best? Is a tree intelligent? Does it know, and how does it know?*

Carl Rogers, a twentieth century psychologist, recounts how, as a young boy, he saw some weird-looking shoots in the cellar of his home. He realised they came from a bin of potatoes stored for the winter. There was a small window in the cellar, the potatoes had sprouted and were reaching toward the only light available. In better conditions the potatoes would throw up strong, green shoots rather than such white, spindly shoots. Rogers reflected: "We can say that there is in every organism, at whatever level, an underlying flow of movement toward constructive fulfilment of its intrinsic possibilities ... the actualizing tendency." He continued: "Whether we are speaking of a flower or an oak tree, of an earthworm or a beautiful bird, of an ape or a person, we will do well, I believe, to recognize that life is an active process not a passive one" (Rogers, 1996, pp. 117-118). What Rogers deduced from his observations was an organism's inherent intelligence and capacity to harness its ways of knowing in order to reach toward its potential. Since Rogers wrote, scientific understanding of sentience and intelligence has changed considerably. We now realise humans find it difficult to recognise intelligence unless it resembles our own; hence we have been blind to its expression in other living organisms.

Sentience and intelligence as ways of knowing

Recently researchers have begun to perceive intelligence more widely as the capacity to sense or gather information through different ways of knowing and use that to respond to the external environment. Mancuso and Viola observed recently: "Plants are highly responsive, attuned to gravity, grains of sand, sunlight, starlight, the footfalls of tiny insects and to slow rhythms outside our range. They are subtle, aware, strategic beings whose lives involve an environmental sensitivity very distant from the simple flower and seed factories of popular imagination" (Mancuso & Viola, 2015). Although they have no brain they are capable of a wide range of adaptive responses and indeed may 'choose' between stimuli in their environment to select the one that will best support their capacity to become. They have a distributed and sophisticated array of what Mancuso and Viola call "tiny computing structures" that give off the same signals as neurons in an animal brain and work together to form a responsive network. A tree, such as the one I observed in the Woodbrooke garden, is sentient and intelligent in terms of its capacity to gather information from its internal and external environment.

Plants also communicate. Karban researched plant sensing and communication and established that plants process information, sense their environment and strive to optimise their conditions. Plants respond to the position of competitors and availability of resources. Their decisions are influenced by past experience, akin to memory, and they respond to reliable cues to future events and anticipate accordingly. They are able to distinguish and respond between close relatives and strangers. Karban also established that plants are in what he called "lively and constant discourse" with each other, especially nearby kin and they develop co-operative behaviour. (Karban, 2015) It seems there is a sense in which trees, as examples of plants, are, in their own way, capable of making decisions for the best.

An ecology of ways of knowing

Trees are living systems that occupy a critical niche in the web of relationships that comprise our planet. We humans are part of the same ecological system. The world revealed by ecology and quantum science tells us that our physical reality is an undivided oneness at both the systemic and quantum levels.

But when I look at another living species do I see it as made of the same stuff that I am made? If all life is blessed with the capacity to strive to fulfil its potential, is there any sense in which other species are spirit-led? Is it the same energy, field, loving, wise and compassionate presence? And if physical reality is an undivided oneness, spiritually, what narrative encompasses this understanding? How might we perceive the Inward Light, the Spirit or essence of trees, and if this is not specific to trees then what might this imply about the interiority of spirit in all things? What are the 'clothes' God wears?

Reflections – source and Source

- The language and approach taken in Theory U is secular and does not employ religious or spiritual language. Yet in other ways it is intrinsically spiritual in its understanding and use of source as the root of presence and inner knowing.

- God is an unusual word in today's usage. Most words have a broad but agreed shared meaning so communication is possible, e.g. the word 'chair' may cover a wider range of actual chairs but is imbued with sufficient general recognition of its form and purpose that the word has meaning. 'God' is different because it no longer has (if it ever had) an assigned, common meaning; the meaning you assign to God may be different to what others think you mean, or indeed they mean, but this is not evident without a conversation that is frequently difficult to have; the discomfort leads people to adopt various words or phrases that denote what God is for them without any common agreement as to meaning.

- For some for whom God is the most accurate language and reflection of their spiritual experience, Jaworski's perception of Source will be too distant from their notion of God. There will be others for whom his description differs from their personal experience but is familiar and thought-provoking.

- Jaworski's concept of Source embraces numerous ideas current in spirituality in the early decades of the twenty-first century. His concept of Source is congruent with Eastern traditions, particularly Taoism. It resonates with a drift away from established Christian understanding toward a more free-floating spirituality that eschews conventional notions of God. Liebert came across Theory U as she wrote about the Social Discernment Cycle used in her community and teaching. She observes striking resonances and complementarity between this Cycle and Theory U. And she criticises Theory U for its apparent lack of familiarity with Western spirituality and lack of grounding in contemplative practice. Meaning has been found instead through secularised variants of Eastern traditions. Liebert points out that source in the Christian tradition would include "the indwelling of the Holy Spirit, in which the Christian believer would understand that the source of life and wisdom is already within (but not reduced to) all of creation" (Liebert, 2015, pp. 170-174). Elsewhere I have tried to include God-based expressions of source by writers who, like Liebert, are at ease with God language within a broad, inclusive and creative spiritual framework of experience and belief.

- Whatever notion of source speaks to you, in making decisions for the best – being discerning – it is essential we are clear about the standard to which we hold ourselves accountable in determining what represents for the best. The need for continuing self-reflection, and practices such as daily reflection – for example Experiment with Light and Examen respectively – are necessary steps to both self-knowledge and learning to recognise and surrender with integrity to discerning the movements of spirit and the creative presence that we may name as God.

- We do well to recall, in the words of Hewitson: "We are all caught in the net of history, culture and family, all of these influencing us in ways beyond our awareness. Western thoughtframes are simply that – a limited perspective on the world. And sometimes these are not effective lenses for seeing God's presence" (Hewitson, 2013 p. 17).

Chapter 7. Crystallising: from clerking to enacting

Theory U explains crystallising as clarifying vision and intention whilst staying true to the connection with source and inner knowing that arises. The purpose and essence of crystallising is to clarify and put into words what the individual or group wants to create, what wants to emerge. The act of crystallising activates the power of intention, and even when there are setbacks, in the Quaker phrase, we trust that 'way opens'. Letting go is balanced by letting come, attuning to the flow of what is to be done.

At this point in a U process, we face the question of how to act on this opening for the creative process of Spirit to manifest and evolve through us. In a general sense, acting on our discernment is an opportunity, as George Fox put it, to "Be patterns, be examples in all countries, places, islands, nations, wherever you come, that your carriage and life may preach among all sorts of people, and to them; then you will come to walk cheerfully over the world, answering that of God in every one" (QFP 2016, para 1.02).

As the movement into the curve of the U marked a threshold – going through the eye of the needle – so we pass through another threshold now. What must we each do to harness mind and heart in activating our will to be a pattern in the world? A simple daily period of reflection and connecting with source, opening to the Light, upholds and keeps us connected with this inner unity.

As my enquiry engages with its final movement, going up, I illustrate crystallising and acting on our discernment with vignettes from Quaker-led or Quaker-inspired organisations. All the vignettes arose by chance rather than design. Whilst I was carrying out my research I had conversations where I explaining what I was doing and, as the person I was with told me about their current work, they illustrated exactly what I was looking at. I use them to bring life and real-life examples to my work.

Discerning as a precise stage in decision-making

As a Quaker meeting for corporate decision-making becomes gathered, I perceive two parallel and reciprocal inward motions at work: all those present are increasingly thinking and sensing as a whole rather than simply as separate individuals, and those present are in oneness with the movement of spirit, with God. The discernment is perceived as the inner knowing of all present and the role of the clerk is to sense the meeting reaching this state of unity. With and on behalf of the group, the clerk begins to crystallise this inner knowing into words; the precise stage of discernment as the clerk begins to draft a minute. Once drafted it is offered to the meeting so all can participate in fine-tuning both the detail of the discernment and how it is expressed in words. Although there is 'a clerk', I see clerking as an activity of the whole group, not simply the clerk. The meeting reaches unity when all present are content that the minute faithfully articulates the inner knowing of the group as it can best discern the matter at that time. The meeting reaches unity and has an agreed minute articulating and recording its discerned decision. Quakers are unusual but not unique in recording their minutes at the time; it can be both a remarkable process and one that is desperately difficult[10].

I was present at a Quaker business meeting when the meeting was getting bogged down in discerning its way forward. The clerk suggested we deal with other business and return to this later. When we returned to it, there was little further discussion, I don't recall a clear direction emerging, but the clerk offered to try a minute. As the meeting upheld the clerk in worship I had an image of the contributions made to discussion floating above the clerk's head. Some were being guided down through her writing hand. The clerk read the minute and asked for any further discernment of the draft; no-one spoke. The minute was accepted at it stood. I was left with a graphic image representing what I might imagine was happening as the minute was drafted.

A reflection on leadership

In observing what he called 'renewal leadership' Jaworski noted: "At the heart of this kind of performance is a capacity for accessing tacit knowing that can be used for breakthrough thinking, envisioning and creating the kind of world we desire." This relates, to my mind,

---

[10] Much could be written about meetings that don't reach or are not in unity but it is not my purpose to explore this here

to the role of clerking. Clerking offers subtle leadership in service of the meeting. Quaker commitment to equality and justice tests the notion of leadership. There is acute sensitivity toward the power, rank and status that comes with a position or role. Different ideas of leadership, such as servant leadership or distributed leadership, are more acceptable as they exercise power with, rather than power over, others. As a society, we have limited experience of enabling shared leadership and responsibility in the workplace. We have more familiarity with such methods in small groups. It requires integrity, sensitivity and skill to lead wisely.

Wilson wrote about authority, leadership and concern, noting that it embraced moral authority, e.g. crystallising vision and intention into a discerned decision, and administrative authority, e.g. where someone is charged with transmitting the decision to others and turning it into action. Wilson drew on his experience in Quaker relief work during and after the Second World War (Wilson, 2007). The principal ideas I wish to take from his 1949 Swarthmore Lecture are his understanding of the ethos and nature of organisations and the distinction between moral and administrative authority. Wilson described the ethos and nature of organisations as "a corporate body capable of both common-sense and imaginative action, combined with a natural ability to convey to others a sense of inner peace and stability, surviving outward chaos and yet not divorced from it" (Wilson, 2007, p. 19). He observed the complex arrangements in Quaker organisations that wrestled with being grounded in their Quaker faith and answerable to Quaker structures yet "able to act with the precision and certainty of a well-run business". He concluded: "To determine what shall be done and the quality of the spirit in which ends shall be pursued, is a moral responsibility; to determine how that shall be done and to see that it is done, is an administrative responsibility within the moral framework. Moral responsibility is found by Friends through 'the sense of the Meeting'." Administrative responsibility in complex matters is taken by individuals given the task of translating 'the sense of the Meeting' into action, being guided all along by the moral obligation to remain true to 'the sense of the Meeting'." (Wilson, 2007, pp. 32-45). Wilson's view is echoed in today's *Quaker Faith & Practice*: "It is neither possible nor desirable for every Friend to take a detailed interest in the work of every committee. We are, however, called to a broad sympathy with, and understanding of, the extent of the work entrusted to the committees under the guidance of Meeting for Sufferings in the name of the whole yearly meeting" (QFP, 2016 para 8.24). As I turn to Quaker-led and Quaker-inspired organisations as my practical examples, Wilson's distinctions are as valid now as when they were written.

Leadership: translating between moral and administrative authority

Leadership is an essential element in crystallising vision and intent, and translating the vision and intent articulated in a discerned decision into action. Skilful and wise leadership is needed especially when those who make a decision concrete and real in the world are not part of the circle discerning the decision. They need to trust the discernment process which shapes their daily life in an organisation, and when they hold responsibility for working out what is done to turn a discerned decision into a programme of work. Leadership is not restricted to roles such as senior management; true leadership is shared wherever people have a capacity to see how they can make a difference. Another key element in translating discernment into action lies in relationships – between people in different roles in an organisation, between an organisation and those it serves, between an organisation and its external environment, stakeholders and partners.

The spirit of Woodbrooke Quaker Study Centre – a vignette

Sitting in a Meeting for Worship at Woodbrooke, I wondered yet again what the difference is between a number of people meditating together and a Quaker Meeting for Worship. As I noted that everyone present was united by a connection to Woodbrooke, I sensed this as a central vision and intent carried forward from Woodbrooke's founding impulse. It continues through the stewardship of those translating that founding vision and intent into fruition today. I thought of it as the Spirit of Woodbrooke, and its current mission "Quality Service, Quaker Values" seemingly seeps out of the walls.

I have long felt that organisations have a soul or spirit. I interpret this as their founding impulse running as a thread through time, a focusing force for its action in the world. I find some organisations recognise this or something similar as their angel; Walter Wink, a noted Christian nonviolent activist, perceived spirituality as "the 'interiority' — or 'angel' — of people, institutions and even nations" (McIntosh, 2008). The responsibility given to those associated with an organisation is to uphold this thread, discern what it means now, what faithfully expresses that impulse in the world and how it is carried out. I wondered whether senior management in an organisation discern and work with their sense of the spirit of the organisation and how this affects their work. I met Sandra Berry, Director of Woodbrooke, to discuss this aspect of her role.

Discernment and moral authority

Sandra told me the Spirit of Woodbrooke is real to her. It is alive, for example, through Woodbrooke's ministry of hospitality; it speaks through people's stories of Woodbrooke and is kept alive by new stories and memories that she likens to creating new synapses and neural pathways in the 'organisational brain'. Sandra also used an analogy of the work of Woodbrooke as the sails of a ship that allows the wind of the Spirit of Woodbrooke to move.

Woodbrooke trustee meetings (it is a registered charity) use Quaker business method, which Sandra sees as the outward sign that discernment is the way the business works. It is 'informed discernment', an approach resonant with the U process: gathering views, ideas and opinions from a wide range of points of view; there are multiple possibilities; discernment searches for that which feels right, seems to offer a possibility for the best and feels right in relation to the Spirit of Woodbrooke. Once a decision is discerned, "waiting doesn't help and we will review how it turns out". An open will is essential – "a discerned decision may be outside what you've thought of and you need an open will to accept and go with it". Looking at the U map, Sandra currently sees the organisation at the bottom of the U, a place of possibilities emerging.

Discernment is tested by people's feedback. People are the mainstay of the centre's work. Coming to Woodbrooke nurtures them in a deep way and the ministry of hospitality is not 'fluffy'. Measuring their impact tells the organisation if they are getting it right.

Leadership

Sandra's model is servant leadership but she accepts that in her role she holds ultimate responsibility. Wilson's distinction between moral and administrative responsibility can be observed in the balance between the roles of trustee and director. At Woodbrooke both hold moral responsibility but administrative responsibility is held primarily by the director and staff. Sandra aims to value and empower the best in people: "A team isn't a group of people who work together; it's a group who trust each other." Woodbrooke has to be resilient and adaptable, able to work with change therefore staff work across boundaries. Nevertheless, her role brings responsibility for ensuring everyone works toward the same vision, enabling the right structure for the spirit, place and people of Woodbrooke to flourish.

Making the connection and bridging between a discerned decision and all those working at Woodbrooke requires care. It is a mixed Quaker and non-Quaker staff and she finds what works is sitting together, talking openly and listening together – discernment without needing to express it in terms some may find uncomfortable. Sandra has her own personal discernment practice, listening for what she feels and thinks is the way to act in putting trustees' discernment faithfully into practice. She will sit quietly and listen inwardly to herself; ask "where am I listening in myself?"; letting the matter run through her, noting what seems to be driving her decisions especially where she is aware of uncomfortable emotions such as anger. She will also make sure she spends time in the outdoors as "the physical connects you differently, it stops you over-thinking".

Theory U recognises that crystallising vision and intention requires a context that nurtures and is sympathetic to this way of working. Sandra's description of how she perceives and uses leadership at Woodbrooke to translate discernment into action demonstrates one example of a nurturing context.

Reflections: sense of the meeting, clerking, from discernment to action

- Jane Mace considered 'the sense of the meeting', quoting Morley's reminder that this refers to early Quakers' understanding of ongoing revelation. Sense of the meeting, in Morley's view, ensues from a process of release of feelings and opinions, a long focus of broader, wider attention, and the enveloping harmony of turning towards the Light (Mace, 2012, pp. 43-44). Mace's exploration of sense of the meeting seems to signify an inner knowing that emerges in a context of those present being in unity in being present to and sensing God's presence and bringing it present in the world.

- At the start, I noted that the word discernment is used in three ways, one being to indicate a precise stage in decision-making. In this usage, discernment is the specific means by which Quakers collectively act in seeking the will of God and being spirit-led. It is mediated through the activity of clerking which is responsive to the sense of the meeting held collectively by all present. The activity of clerking and the contemporaneous recording of discernment in a minute are greatly valued. There are variants in the way clerking is practised, e.g. co-clerking where two people share the role between them, and it is flexible enough to be performed in various ways. One difficulty is drafting a complex minute; with a smallish group I have experimented with what I think of as 'collaborative clerking': the group as a whole discerns the sub-headings as a guide to the flow and detail a minute requires before the clerk drafts the content of a minute in the normal way. In some places, groups (not necessarily Quaker) are becoming skilled in using electronic means, such as white boards or a laptop, to write contemporaneous minutes that a group read and discern in recording their agreement.

- I have wondered whether sensing and checking personal discernment, clarifying my discernment in words I can continue to reflect on, is a variant of clerking that I think of as self-clerking. Gerald Hewitson talks about our inner clerk "that voice which takes soundings of all our internal competing voices, and emerges with a firm measured clarity, offering a purposeful sense of direction" (Hewitson, 2013, p. 12). I might also liken it, at its most profoundly spirit-led, as what the New Testament and other writers explore as putting on the Mind of Christ.

- Clerking is heavily identified with a role in Quaker life. If I look at it as an activity rather than a role, then I find it a rich blend. In an organisation or group it is a nexus of care, upholding and enabling: of discernment, of the interior activity of being and acting from an inward place – opening to the Light and allowing inner knowing to emerge as a way of being – and connection with an intangible overseeing spirit, angel or soul. I found the role of clerk of trustees of a UK charity that was also a Quaker-inspired organisation fascinating. The role calls for blending the Quaker spirituality of the role, being chair of trustees, therefore a lead role for the organisation's statutory, legal and societal responsibility and a chair of meetings. Thus, the preparation for the meeting might require much reading and mastering the detail of the business; being chair required oversight of our performance in the charitable domain; being clerk required different preparation. I understood how coming with heart and mind prepared gives rise to the Quaker phrase "praying the papers" and I came to learn more of the inward relationship with the spirit of an organisation. As I spoke with Sandra Berry I sensed this nexus again.

- I find that Quaker ways of crystallising vision and intention, and Berry's account of translating discernment into action, are consistent with the overall U map. Quaker practice adds practical steps that, in the language of Theory U, operate from deeper inner place. The overall impact of this on the depth and rigour of Quaker discernment is to make it, at its best, authentically "an exercise of listening to God through what each person says" (Mace,2012. p136, quoting Gillman) as well as a collective act of meeting for worship for attending to business.

Chapter 8. Prototyping and Performing: testing and developing discernment by doing

I referred earlier to Arthur's insight that: "Every profound innovation is based on an inward-bound journey, on going to a deeper place where knowing comes to the surface" and the consequent phase of acting swiftly with a natural flow. The initial test of discernment proposed in Theory U is to design a prototype that translates discernment into action. Once trialled, the prototype is reviewed; this checks that the discernment was valid and the action faithfully reflects its intention. The first cycle of a U process is completed as the action is modified to effectively marry the intention with the context, needs and resources of the situation; it is performed in the world. In this chapter I explore prototyping and performing through three more vignettes.

Theory U describes prototyping and performing as co-creation. I visualise this as four nested bubbles: an innermost bubble holding inner knowing; from which arises a bubble upholding the best that is possible in a situation; leading to a prototype action which experiments with a microcosm of a way forward; the fourth bubble is the fulfilled expression of the action as good work in the world (see diagram 18 on the next page).

Discernment is brought into being through doing and, in Quaker terms, in trust that "Way opens" as a prototype emerges. Initially, action as doing is an unknown. However much care goes into what Sandra called 'informed discernment', until the idea of an action is tried we cannot know how it will work in the external environment and with such resources of people, finance and imagination available; the point of prototyping is to be experimental, an approach Quakers value. Once tried, successive iterations tweak or re-design the implementation. If the initiative proves feasible and useful it can be scaled up and shared where it is needed; this is performing, the final stage in the movement going up the U. Theory U adds that action integrates head, heart and hands. They argue that this unity of head, heart and hands requires ongoing connection to source through reflective practice, staying true and connected with the deeper vision and intention.

Diagram 18: prototyping and performing as co-creation

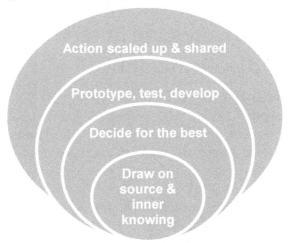

Furthermore, taking action demands that you pay attention – listening, being willing to take risks from your highest self, and act in good timing. The final product incorporates all of the best and most appropriate features of the prototype. The discerned action is seen in the context of the wider system, its place in the shape of things, the web of relationships. The individual sees the meaning of their work in the web of relationships.

In one sense, none of this is news in the context of Quaker discernment but setting it out clearly can help codify Quaker practice. In Quaker practice, testing the validity of the discernment is a key step and prototyping a means of doing so. From a practical point of view, prototyping checks how well an idea works in situ and whether the resources are available and appropriate. At a deeper level, actually putting the discernment into action and paying attention to what happens is itself a form of discernment that combines practical demonstration with constant inward monitoring and reflection. Is the action still an accurate perception of inner knowing? Is inner knowing adapting itself to the flow of life?

Prototyping – a learned and learning organisational skill

This vignette comes from Quaker Social Action (QSA)[11]. For nearly 150 years QSA has taken action against poverty with practical

---

[11] www.quakersocialaction.org.uk/

projects tested in East London. QSA's particular skill lies in identifying niche impacts of poverty on people's lives and finding ways to help those affected address them – prototyping. In recent years it has grown its skill and capacity to disseminate, share and train up others to deliver a similar service themselves in their locality – performing. A New Philanthropy Capital assessment of QSA noted: "QSA is not afraid to experiment and be creative, and the charity puts a lot of thought into developing and piloting innovative services—for example, QSA is a leader in financial education for families. This creativity means that QSA is not afraid to take risks and try new approaches. These new approaches however also come with a lot of careful planning, and QSA makes a great effort to measure its impact so it can learn from what is successful and what is less so" (NPC; 2009).

The majority of QSA trustees, and specifically the clerk, are required to be Quakers and care is taken to induct non-Quaker trustees in Quaker business method as the method by which trustees, with the director, Judith Moran, discern their decisions. As with Sandra in the previous vignette, Judith as director is responsible for turning a discerned decision into a project that fits QSA's mission and charitable aims, is congruent with its way of working and addresses an issue on which QSA has some expertise. In this vignette Judith describes how QSA planned its first ever lobbying campaign and her role in setting out the activities QSA wished to see within the campaign and the tone and characteristics of how it would campaign.

In 2013, trustees decided to develop a national funeral poverty campaign and fundraise to publicise and lobby on the issue and launch a fair funerals pledge for funeral directors to endorse. By October 2015, within two years from the original discernment, QSA's Fair Funerals Campaign[12] was named by *The Guardian* national newspaper as campaign of the month, noting: "There aren't many campaigns underway that have achieved both significant cross-party support and, in just over a year, made lasting changes to an industry. Charities could learn a great deal from the apolitical moves made by QSA."

---

[12] www.fairfuneralscampaign.org.uk/

Trustees' discernment built on an earlier decision to design an intervention to address the problem of people on a low income falling into debt because of the high cost of paying for a funeral for a loved member of the family. Prototyping *Down to Earth* had taken much patience and commitment throughout the organisation to successfully turn a discerned decision into a sustainable and viable project. It demonstrated ongoing testing of a discerned decision as trustees and Judith kept checking back that, despite the initial challenges, the proposal was still in accord with the original discernment. As the project found its way and demonstrated the need, QSA saw a new development – to address the issue at its heart, not simply the symptoms of people falling into debt. It grew from a sense that, because of *Down to Earth*, QSA's expertise on funeral poverty was increasingly recognised, thus uniquely placing them to lead a credible campaign on the issue. QSA was awarded funds by both of the trusts who were approached and recruited someone to lead the campaign.

Judith says: "It was clear to me that we had to ensure that the tone of the campaign was aligned with our existing ways of working. Moreover, it felt at the time (and I would say has been proved by experience to date) that this would in fact be a strength and might distinguish us from other campaigns and ultimately lead to the outcomes we wanted to see for people experiencing funeral poverty.

"So, we decided the campaign should be based on our established values of work:

- "*Evidence-based* – to retain credibility and increase our chances of being taken seriously

- "*Positive* – seeking alliances and building allegiances across all sections of government and the funeral industry

- "*Keen to listen* – understanding the position of those we wished to influence, especially within the funeral industry and government

- "*Undertaken in good faith* – that our agenda and the agenda of others might not always overlap but we needed to respect their position

- "*Practical* – always focusing in on what was possible, despite our limited resources.

"This has helped us tremendously. We have been able to keep relationship building with the industry and are taken seriously by all the major players. Journalists come again and again to seek us out, not for the shouty sound-bite but for a considered perspective. We have managed to steer an alliance of over sixty non-profit organisations interested in this subject, without weighty governance arrangements or a flagging of interest."

What this vignette demonstrates is quiet persistence; commitment to the rightness of a discerned decision; confidence that the principle of fair funerals would be best served by campaigning in alignment with the organisation's integrity and values; courage by trustees and trust in the staff, who were aware of the potential reputational risk if this new kind of high-profile, public venture did not work. The values Judith set out above were wholly consistent with the place of Quaker discernment at the heart of QSA. It illustrates good practice and skill in taking a decision from discernment to prototyping and performing: willing to experiment, take risks, stay connected with inner knowing; and consistently be clear about how the organisation might experimentally marry its core values and integrity to a new kind of activity.

Prototyping to performing – integrity between words and action

My next vignette is from Danielle Walker Palmour, director of Friends Provident Foundation (FPF). FPF is a grant-making charitable foundation, set up after Friends Provident Life Office was de-mutualised in 2001 with an endowment from accounts that could not be traced. Its interest is in the right use of money and its current funding programme focuses on contributing to a more resilient, sustainable and fairer economic system[13]. It has a Quaker heritage, however, as Friends Provident Life was originally founded by Quakers and espoused Quaker values; current trustees and staff are committed to the Quaker values written into its governing documents. Currently, Danielle is a Quaker and I am the only Quaker amongst the trustees.

---

[13] www.friendsprovidentfoundation.org/programme-overview/

This vignette illustrates discernment in a small non-Quaker charitable organisation. It also illustrates the role of integrity in designing the development of an organisation, and the questions addressed in carrying a vision into fully embodying its intention. FPF consciously uses prototyping as a means of achieving its charitable and funding aims. Its grant-giving programme funds prototype projects that if successful are capable of being scaled up to develop local and systemic economic resilience. The changes that Danielle describes below show how FPF is deliberately prototyping the way an endowed foundation can embed its core values throughout its activities.

FPF trustees and staff meet as a collaborative group with staff input not only valued but acclaimed for the vital role of their experience and knowledge in the organisation. No votes are taken and decisions are discerned on the basis of an ongoing cycle of reflection, consideration and learning, and measured against the Foundation's values (although in law trustee decision-making is the responsibility of the trustee board). FPF decision-making is congruent with Quaker business method in the sense of coming prepared for the process and giving one's own will up to the discernment of the meeting. The right use of money is a key principle itself not just an aim. The Foundation's endowment has been in ethical investment funds since it was established. Transparency is also important in the organisation, in relationship to grant-holders and stakeholders. One early impetus that gave rise to the changes described came from a grantholder survey that told trustees how much grant-holders valued the contribution from staff in advice, support, challenge, interest and networking; this led trustees to see the importance of leveraging this skill and experience further in support of the Foundation's aims. It is clear that my initial definition of discernment as decisions that are made for the best and for the whole is true in this context.

From 2013-2015 FPF was occupied with establishing its full operational independence but at the same time trustees and staff began to ask some fundamental questions about their work. They also gathered ideas and thoughts from a range of other similar foundations, including some who shared their Quaker origins and interests, size, focus, and innovative approach. The main questions were:

- What is the purpose of the organisation – a question that needs asking again and again?

- Who holds the vision of the organisation?

- Who needs to be involved in discernment, such as trustees, staff, external advisers, grant-holders?

- What are our tools to bring about change?

- What is the role and function of Trustees in relation to: trust of staff, of other stakeholders? Where and on what can trustees add value?

Danielle summarised what happened as trustees and staff considered these questions:

- "The Foundation has three main ways of bringing about change: a) giving grants and social investments; b) more active use of our investments as they are our largest asset; c) convening networks and dialogues and synthesising learning.

- "Our governance structures and staff activity gave preference to grant giving and social investment over other ways of bringing about change and needed to be re-balanced.

- "We needed to build on innovation we found in other places and organisations to suggest new tools that might enable Trustee time to be spent on areas where their insights could be best applied.

- "Staff as professionals should take a greater role in the processes of shaping change and trustees needed to work out the boundaries of trust and delegation."

Trustees decided that any changes they made to the organisation would be driven by an over-arching criterion – enabling FPF to more fully and actively walk its talk. The principles of the right use of money, integrity, fairness, equality and transparency must inform everything the Foundation does and the way it does them[14]. Changes would be regarded as experiments and reviewed – prototyped in their own right. Danielle explained the experiments currently being implemented.

---

[14] www.friendsprovidentfoundation.org/about-us/beliefs/

"FPF is bringing in new staff roles. It is resourcing an investment engagement manager to engage in dialogue with companies, investors and charitable networks linked to our concerns. There is a second new role in communications and convening so the Foundation's knowledge and influence is optimised.

"Re-balancing trustees' time so quarterly meetings are less dominated by decisions on grants and more attention given to strategy, dissemination and learning. Trustees are fine-tuning a voting tool to give them an initial scope of outline applications to identify areas needing trustee discussion. Once second stage grant applications have gone through the established staff assessments, staff are tasked to bring forward a portfolio of grants that best support the Foundation's charitable and programme aims so trustee discussion focuses on grant strategy, trends, addressing questions and identifying gaps in the Foundation's grant portfolio.

"Scheduled joint learning sessions including, for instance, input from external presenters, grant-holder sessions, and teach-ins with new staff.

"Inside out reviews as the changes in the Foundation's focus must be reflected in its operations. For instance, the Foundation has a focus and funds work on pay transparency and parity in corporate life. Therefore is the Foundation itself transparent on pay and pay ratios? Another Foundation focus and grant funding is tax avoidance; the Foundation offers staff a salary sacrifice option whereby pension contributions reduce tax payment. Together we are asking ourselves if this is part of a culture of tax avoidance. FPF has become a Living Wage employer and Living Wage Friendly Funder so it can encourage its grant-holders to make any salary funded by a Foundation grant to be paid at the living wage rate too."

Danielle describes a comprehensive programme of change with an overall aim of more closely integrating the Foundation's aims and principles with every aspect of its work. It illustrates a Theory U principle of staying connected to inner knowing by integrating its heart, mind and hands into the changes it is making. It is consciously prototyping how to walk its talk to lead and inspire deeper ethical principles in the charitable sector; putting an organisation on the cutting edge is taking a risk in order to leverage change. FPF also shows how an organisation can make decisions that are congruent with the working definition of discernment used in my enquiry; in this instance, FPF did not necessarily set out to consciously describe themselves in those words but their own practice arose naturally from a culture that is informed by Quaker values and practice and individual trustees are cognisant of this heritage and supportive of it.

Performing – a Quaker organisation using Theory U as a strategic tool

QUNO is an international Quaker United Nations Office working from Quaker houses in New York and Geneva to continue long-standing Quaker work for a more peaceful and just world. It works at the United Nations and with other multinational agencies to pursue Quaker values of patient, quiet diplomacy. QUNO's website says: "The strength of QUNO's work lies in QUNO's long-term persistence. Through perseverance, we have helped to change attitudes, create new understandings, and develop new standards."[15]

Jonathan Woolley is director of the QUNO office in Geneva and I met him to discuss how QUNO Geneva has been using Theory U as one of its tools for planning strategy and discerning areas of work to develop that most effectively deploy its stretched resources in service of its aims. Jonathan told me that before he took up the post in Geneva in 2011, he told a friend about how Quakers decided (discerned) what to work on. The friend exclaimed: "Then Quakers are on the cutting edge of management theory; what you have described is Theory U in practice." With that lead, and the confirmation from staff that they found the concepts useful and practical, QUNO has experimented with Theory U as a planning tool; when QUNO Geneva Committee examined new areas of work, it also looked at how it had discerned its areas of work in the past and how it might do so in its then current review.

This vignette illustrates how an organisation can incorporate Theory U into its work and how it tests the congruence between this method and QUNO's existing use of Quaker discernment. In late 2011, the committee noted: "We have also looked a little at some of the thinking from other fields such as management research about how best to think about the future, including 'learning from the

---

[15] www.quno.org/about

future as it emerges'. A more creative description of discernment, although partly compatible with the model above, comes from a description of how successful teams work for the future. It was developed by Otto Scharmer, Peter Senge and others at MIT and gives the impression that Quakers are on the cutting edge, because we think we do what they describe! It resonates with us as one possible description of how we discover and discern new work (and make adjustments to existing work)" (QUNO Geneva, 2016).

Their record demonstrates an organisation initially working to understand a new tool, thinking it through, and testing it out. Then, over a period of four to five years, they successively used the main framework of Theory U to discern potential new areas of work and map the organisation's portfolio of programmes to give a dynamic overview of its faith in action. They found it useful in helping them to understand where they stood in relation to existing work priorities. Staff and committee members seem to have been satisfied that Theory U combined seamlessly with Quaker discernment.

Initially, Jonathan told me, they learned about the five main phases of a Theory U cycle, noting that it is iterative and not completed in a single cycle. This was gradually adapted to their areas of work. Their notes show staff and the committee thinking through the stages and how their own process matched it, how it cross-referenced the way they saw their work, how they understood its development and its context. They reflected on how the Theory U map related to how they first began to discern what might be new areas of work:

"Sometimes it's QUNO staff that initially perceive a call (stage 1), sometimes it may be a concern received through Friends World Committee for Consultation or through Quaker Meetings and sometimes a mixture of these." They considered what Theory U might suggest to them about future collaboration:

"We should involve Quaker United Nations Committee, sympathetic outside partners and key informants, etc., in the process. If the model is correct, then maybe their role is more in contributing to steps 2, 3 and 4 (listening; reflecting; dreaming prototypes) rather than in conventional analysis." From this review, QUNO Geneva went on to map their areas of work by locating them on a Theory U map as if it mapped the programme's life cycle and, as their notes show, discussing and working out the stage that different projects were at and how that helped them better understand and review the flow and development of their work (Diagram 19).

Diagram 19: Theory U stages applied to QUNO Geneva work, 2012

By 2016, their use of a Theory U map showed the increasingly assured way in which Theory U was becoming part of their analytical and reflective toolkit and strengthening their discernment on their work as it unfolded (see Diagram 20).

Jonathan comments that the most important present use for QUNO of the Theory U map is to accommodate in QUNO's processes work that is at very different stages of development and scales of investment. It allows staff and the committee to be clear in any particular year about which are established (stage 5) or emerging (stage 4) areas of work and which ones are being discerned (stage 1, 2 and 3). It allows the consideration or temporary 'parking' of possible areas of work without losing the discipline that they should be discerned when the right time comes, before making significant investments.

He also points out that the map is used as a reference point for staff and committee on a regular yearly basis rather than as a day-today tool. "We carefully prepare an updated map and refer to it each year in our main discernment meeting with the Committee. But if you monitored us during the year between, you might never hear the U referred to. So it's a powerful and recognised reference point and organizer but not in frequent explicit use. It is, however, implicit in determining the development of each piece of work. I can say to a staff member: "I think we should gather more information about what others are doing before we are ready to propose to the Committee that 'this is for us' and we will both know we are talking about stage 2. It allows nascent ideas and large efforts to co-exist."

Diagram 20: Theory U stages applied to QUNO Geneva work, 2016

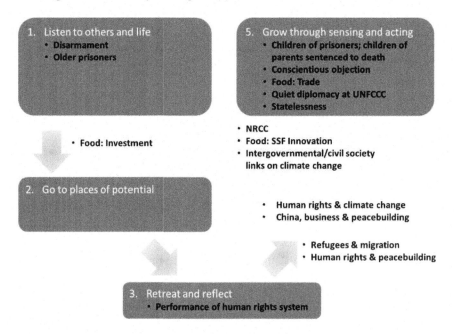

Reflections

- The most striking image to come from this review of the movement going up the U is that QUNO Geneva shows it is possible and helpful to combine their Quaker methods of discernment with a U process. I have heard from a number of those involved in this process of the enthusiasm and insight this gave them. I notice the complementarity between Quaker discernment as deciding for the best and QUNO Geneva applying the principle of "learning from the future as it emerges" to reflect on the future of their own work. This is significant in terms of making the link for Quakers between worship and faith in action.

- "Seeking to live at all times in a divine order of life, Quakers have always counted social service part of Christianity. In fidelity to the genius of their inward experience, they have set themselves the task of developing their own spiritual sensitiveness to the light of truth; and have then resolutely confronted the unawakened conscience of the world with the demands of the new light, and have borne witness to it with undaunted patience. This has resulted in progressive enlightenment for themselves, and in the slow but sure triumph of many of the causes of which they have become champions ... William Charles Braithwaite, 1919" (QFP, para. 23.13).

- Other organisations that embody a spiritual impulse find Theory U useful in mapping a strategic way forward; for instance, the Findhorn Foundation have adapted it to map their discussions and consultations through a current process of change.

Chapter 9: Conclusions

In conclusion I want to look back over my enquiry and draw together the main threads. I hope that what has emerged from using Theory U to explore Quaker discernment may help others understand and practise discernment. I will finish by experimenting with a fuller Quaker U map.

Exploring Quaker discernment through a literature review and Theory U

Many of my reflections and conclusions appear in Reflections sections at the end of each chapter. Here I pick out what I found to be significant and useful insights and ways of looking at Quaker discernment.

General observations

- What I have gained from this research is seeing discernment from a fresh perspective, as if examining it in a new light.

- Whereas Theory U is helpful for clear and structured models, Quaker discernment has a depth and detail that feels both solid and 'deep-reaching'.

- However, in Steere's phrase, they mutually irradiate each other to a useful degree. For instance, Quaker and Theory U perspectives on making decisions for the best employ very different vocabularies. This does not imply that there is a direct equivalence between them but each is rich in its own way. I also observe that the feeling tone of each vocabulary differs, from the older more traditional and sometimes somewhat opaque Quaker language to a more current, academic and secular idiom in Theory U. Time and again I found Theory U described aspects of discernment in language that was powerfully resonant – yet fresh and different. The challenge with Theory U is that as it has developed it has become more complex and the volume of writing on Theory U began to make it more difficult to grasp its essence.

- I found Theory U and Quaker discernment have a common and defining 'heart' – decisions are made in an inward and deeply intuitive manner. Both offer variants to the prevailing rational-analytical model of decision-making that are radical in the context in which they were born. Both approaches test the validity of the decisions made in this more subjective mode so it becomes more robust and resilient and tests the resulting outcomes. Theory U brings structure, fresh eyes and a simple map of the process of discernment; this has some potential in helping codify Quaker discernment. Quaker discernment fills out Theory U with its accumulated wisdom and capacity to hold a central and inward focus. Both are spiritual processes in the sense that they seek to go beyond separated minds and reach decisions from a place of oneness although the nature of that oneness is perceived very differently. Quaker discernment is a consciously spiritual approach whilst Theory U is studiedly secular.

- An initial issue was settling on a working definition of discernment. The phrase "discernment is making decisions for the best" helped root my exploration of discernment in something practical rather than abstract. My amended version that discernment is making decisions for the best for the whole particularly reflected Quaker discernment; it is a remarkable feature of Quaker practice that however vigorously views are held, the deeper phases of discernment are markedly open to whatever decision may become apparent. I do not suggest that "discernment is making decisions for the best" is *the* description of discernment, but it served my purpose well.

From my literature review

- I was surprised to find no single authoritative explanation of British experience of Quaker discernment for such a central element of Quaker practice.

- Loring, Bieber and Liebert's books complement and augment each other's perspectives. They are each different yet seem to build on what each other writer said. It was as if they were each one of Bieber's braids and I could see how closely they wove into one another and enriched each other. I have great respect for Loring's two volumes on *Listening Spirituality*; Bieber's three braids are practical and go deeply into discernment whilst the structure of her book is particularly clear; Liebert's work added a different layer of insight and detail. All three together weave, sift and sort the fabric of discernment.

- I found the Quaker Institute for the Future book *A Quaker Approach to Research: Collaborative Practice and Communal Discernment* describes how "the methods developed by Quakers for spirit-led governance could be adapted for spirit-led research". The book shares their creative and valuable applications of Quaker discernment.

Theory U

- At one level I find Theory U simple. I also found some further iterations and detail hard to grasp. Yet I have no doubt Theory U embodies the essence of discernment. I stripped away detail and complexity that was not essential for my purpose. There is far more to Theory U than appears in my text.

- Arthur's original insight about making decisions by reference to inner knowing described it as three movements – going down, going across and going up. I see this offering a succinct yet potent visual overview that represents the flow of a Quaker discernment in a fresh way. Scharmer observed barriers that inhibit free movement through the whole cycle, whether initiating a cycle of discernment – the top left hand of the U – to accessing a deep inner place open to an inner knowing that informs a decision; identifying these barriers is a crucial observation. Extending this to incorporate opening mind, heart and will as elements of a U process shines a light on some of the challenges of skilful discernment. As a practical tool, when I notice my own obstacles to opening, it reminds me to explore my resistance and prompts me to actively suspend, re-direct and let go to move through resistance and engage with opening.

- As I dug deeper into Theory U I appreciated its call that action comes from a whole and integrated self – mind, heart and hands /body in unison, not simply for ourselves but particularly as a means by which we stay in connection with source and inspire action. These, and similar, insights are within Quaker discernment but meeting them in Theory U then made them more evident when I turned back to Quaker discernment.

- Similarly Theory U's explanation of deepening levels of listening and how this opens us toward source and inner knowing amplifies my understanding of Quaker listening. Outward and inward listening is one of the most important dimensions of all models of discernment. It is equally well and differently explained by Loring, Bieber and Liebert, for instance; yet, the structured perception of the four levels of listening give me an overview that enhanced Quaker and spirit-led descriptions of listening.

- I found the Theory U expression "the inner place from which we operate" a potent reminder of this prerequisite in making decisions for the best. Whilst the importance of the inner place from which we operate is fundamental in Quaker discernment, this phrase from Theory U resonates in the mind and heart. It graphically pinpoints the individual and corporate inner work on which Quaker discernment depends if we are to discern effectively and with integrity. Drawing attention to "the blind spot from which we operate" sharpens my appreciation of the resilience of Quaker values, norms and practices that subtly instil the culture that anchors the integrity of Quaker discernment. I wonder, however, if its very familiarity means some Quakers don't always see it clearly.

- I wanted to use Theory U to explore different language about discernment. I find different words give me a new way to get inside something. Much Quaker language about discernment, as Hewitson (p4) and Ambler (Experiment with Light Network, 2016) have observed, is not in the language of today. This makes it harder to grasp, especially when Quakers can no longer assume that Quaker practice is learned almost by osmosis from childhood. Moreover, if language hinders our capacity to discuss discernment amongst ourselves we will struggle to make it real to others. In Theory U the terms Source and inner knowing are not really defined but they point toward a recognisable experience that is not dependent on words such as God and Spirit. Nevertheless, whilst this language has become a stumbling block for some Quakers, it is possible that using secular language is as much an impediment for others. Clearly the words used in Theory U are no more or less neutral than any other, but they are not in common currency in Quaker conversation therefore may encourage more detachment amongst us. My hope is that different language creates a less charged space in which we can accept that each person's language reflects the reality and meaning of their spiritual experience and, as such, it enriches the whole.

- I observed earlier my surprise that downloading in Theory U is seen in quite a negative light. I emphasise the value of seeing downloading as the point at which we consciously recognise and gather everything we bring to a process of discernment. By contrast, in one early conversation, a colleague commented that Quakers sometimes behave as if facts might get in the way of true discernment and waiting on the spirit. The initial gathering of everything that we bring to discernment is important. We can build in a pause to sift and notice which are necessary facts, information, knowledge, feeling and experience and what is unhelpful recycling of unexamined clutter brought forward from the past; the latter needs to be addressed or, as Quakers would say, left outside the door.

Quaker discernment and the U map

- I find the U map helps me to grasp the shape and movement of discernment in a way that words do not. It tells me something about the flow of Quaker worship and discernment that makes Quaker discernment clearer. There is an intuitive flow of energy in the map that I find useful. Simply perceiving a Quaker discernment process as going down to reach a place of resting in one's centre, an experience of stillness, in which we can experience Spirit and from where we can become aware of the promptings of love and truth, and then carry that back into action in the world is, from my point of view, a powerful overview.

- I had food for thought as people suggested how they would like to re-draw the U map. One person suggested the U should be drawn as a firework, particularly a Catherine wheel; many, if not most, of us can recall Quaker business meetings that felt all too much like this. There were suggestions to complete the U across the top to make it an O; as the vignette about QUNO Geneva points out, discernment is often an iterative process, with one discernment leading to a further cycle as a decision needs to be refined or fine-tuned. However, at present I conclude the U map is valid in using a U for the purpose of showing Arthur's three movements. It simply maps a single cycle – and some decisions are complete on a single cycle but many are not. Moreover, if I see each discernment as a U, rather than an O shape, it reminds me that, even if the same matter is being discerned again, each cycle calls for fresh discernment.

Combining Theory U and Quaker discernment

As I conclude my enquiry I want to build a more complex visual representation of Quaker discernment that sums up my learning by:

- Using Arthur's original perception of accessing inner knowing that Scharmer and Jaworski represented as three movements through a letter U

- Overlaying a U map with what I have also learned during my enquiry about Quaker discernment.

I develop this in two stages. Firstly, I re-work the U map using essentially the language and lens of Theory U. I supplement it with descriptions that reflect my understanding of discernment through their language and image. Secondly, I then use essentially the same diagram but replace the language and concepts of Theory U with language and concepts from Quaker discernment. I hope this will sum up what I learned about Quaker discernment, enriched with the imagery and perspective of Theory U and my various writers and voices.

Developing my own U map

Early in my enquiry I identified four strands, based on Arthur's original concept that developed into Theory U. The four strands summed up guidelines for discerning effectively and with integrity. The strands keep our discernment facing toward connecting with, or resting in, source and accessing an inner knowing; I take these to correspond to the ground of Quaker discernment in making decisions for the best for the whole:

- *Opening* mind, heart and will to support a central purpose of

- *Resting* in the deepest inner place or source I can access and allowing an inner knowing to emerge. This is dependent on

- *Listening* to distinguish between the many voices that are heard. Listening does not mean only aural listening to outward voices but embraces a wide range of ways of paying attention to both outward and inward place from which the discerner and discernment function, thus

- *Paying attention* to the inner place from which I – and a group – operate.

In the diagram below I incorporate these strands more as I believe they actually happen – mutually interdependent, and in combination – rather than as discrete steps. It is important to stress that opening takes place outwardly and inwardly (although the emphasis between outward and inward flow at different stages is difficult to show in a diagram). In going down the emphasis is on opening inwardly whilst in going up the emphasis is perhaps more on keeping mind, heart and will open and in unison thus opening outwardly.

Diagram 21: a revised Theory U map

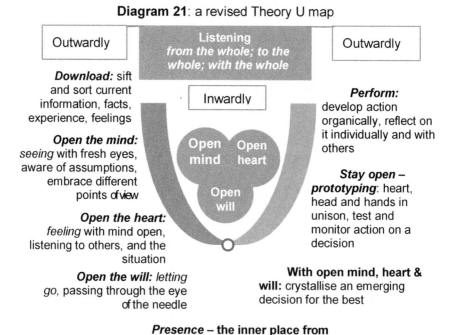

Quaker discernment through the eyes of Theory U

In diagram 22 (next page), I amalgamate a U map such as the one above with Quaker practice and language. The purpose is to present Quaker discernment on a U map; this is a detailed visual account of some principal elements in Quaker discernment shown as movements on a U map.

Diagram 22: a flow of Quaker discernment as a U map

Outwardly	Listening	Outwardly
	For the best: from the whole: for the whole	

Inwardly

Circles: Stilling, Opening, Waiting

Centre down: gather and be present to current information, facts, knowledge, feelings and experience; sift and sort 'wheat from chaff'

Come with heart and mind prepared: willing to *see* with fresh eyes, notice your own limiting views; embrace different opinions

Open heart and mind to function as one: broaden attention, listen to others, and the situation. Consider using threshing or clearness

Open the will: *letting go* to pass through the eye of the needle, leave personal agenda at the door to *let in* the Light

Wait in the Light – the inner place from which we operate: focused on inward being (that of God within), immersed in present moment, empty to self, paying attention to inner knowing

Faithful to discernment in action: evolve organically; nurture potential; trust; reflect on continuing sense of rightness individually and with others

Way opens – *heart, mind & will stay open in unison* – *prototype*: faithfully trial how a decision can be enacted; test and monitor its rightness to discernment and context

Being spirit-led – *letting come with open mind, heart & will* to discern: crystallise, clarify personal direction or clerk a decision, compiled as a meeting reaches unity

117

"Don't let 'the best' drive out 'the good'"

A Spawforth

The Quaker U map on the previous page incorporates the principal elements I have tracked through my enquiry:

- Arthur's three movements – going down, going across and going up – presented visually on a letter U by Scharmer and Jaworski

- The strands I identified in Theory U that also act as underpinning themes in Quaker discernment:

    * *Opening* mind, heart and will to support a central purpose of

    * *Resting* in the deepest inner place or source I can access thus allowing inner knowing to emerge. This is dependent on

    * *Listening* to distinguish between the many voices that are 'heard'; listening as more than aural listening and includes a wide range of different ways of 'listening' and

    * *Paying attention* to the inner place from which I – and a group – operate.

Of course, nothing is as neat or separated as a diagram suggests. The territory we traverse in discernment is messier, more complex, dynamic, and multi-layered. It is, in the end, intangible and beyond linear description. But the point of my enquiry is not to suggest that it is exactly as depicted in a diagram; but presenting Quaker discernment visually can enhance our understanding thus support the integrity and effectiveness of our practice.

I am confident there is sufficient resonance between Quaker discernment and the U map to make it a useful tool to explore and understand the practice of Quaker discernment.

Concluding observations

The vital strand that was clear from the start of my enquiry, and remained present throughout is the depth and feeling for truth that is the heart of Quaker discernment. It is a crucial element in bringing discernment into relationship with the divine. This can be expressed in other ways but what matters is the experience.

What I have gained from studying Theory U and accounts of Quaker discernment is a useful visual stimulus for reflection-in-action – thinking about and noticing what is happening during discernment as it happens – and for thinking about it afterwards – reflection-on-action. My maps and notes are provisional; as my enquiry into Quaker discernment through the eyes of Theory U is shared, I hope there will be comments and contributions that take it forward.

Taking Quaker discernment and Theory U as two examples, it would be hard to weigh up whether we find ourselves looking at differing manifestations of one common experience or at what point they are, in fact, different things. I choose, however, simply to take what I have identified as useful to me in enhancing my understanding of Quaker discernment. To that extent I find the map, the key concepts and practices discussed above, helpful in clarifying my understanding of what is happening in Quaker discernment. I also find it useful in drawing my attention to using discernment more skilfully and upholding the integrity with which it has been handed down. But I also believe that we cannot assume that it will continue to live unless we find ways to talk about discernment and pass on its gifts as more people come fresh to Quakers.

When I started this research, I believed Quaker discernment is a gift to share beyond Quaker circles. My enquiry helped me understand its strength and wisdom. The point about discernment is whether we can use it well so it helps us listen to, and act from, the inner essence of Quaker faith. As Jonathan recounted, at QUNO Geneva, people saw themselves using Quaker discernment and it turned out to be what Theory U describes. And as Hewitson said in his 2013 Swarthmore Lecture: "The searching that leads an inner reorientation of our way of being, [is] based on a sense of loving purpose for our lives. We cannot reach this place using the power of our minds, for it is beyond the level of our surface thinking. It involves us on work on our hearts. It will also involve us in some work on our minds, and the way we see things ... we must penetrate far beyond mere thought, the world constructed by our minds, if we are to engage with our deepest self, our Inner Clerk, and thereby with our Higher Power. As we move towards wholeness we find that completeness, that integrity, for which we were intended" (Hewitson, 2013 p. 24).

And, as you reach the end of my enquiry, I suggest you complete your reflection by returning to the questions I gave at the end of the first chapter (see next page) and consider them afresh in the light of what you have read. This will enable you to see whether your understanding of Quaker discernment has changed in the light of what you have read.

- What does discernment mean to you?

- What practices help you develop skilful discernment?

- How do you experience the inner knowing at the heart of your discernment?

- How do you 'communicate' with this source?

- How do you discern its 'voice'?

- How do you test and act on this?

*"The outer work can never be small if the inner work is great.
And the outer work can never be great if the inner work is small."*
Meister Eckhart

Bibliography

Adams, A. (2012). *Is There Not a New Creation - the experience of early Friends?* Applegarth Publications.

Ambler, R. (2013). *The Light Within Then and Now*. Pendle Hill Pamphlet 425. Pendle Hill Publications.

Arthur, W Brian, in conversation with Jaworski, Scharmer and Jusela. (1999). The Presencing Institute, Retrieved August 18th, 2016, from https://www.presencing.com/sites/default/files/Arthur-1999.pdf

Bache, C. M. (2008). *The Living Classroom – teaching and collective consciousness*. State University of New York Press.

Benefiel, M. (2005). *Soul at Work* (1st edition, Kindle ed.). Seabury Books.

Berry, S. (2016, August 20). A conversation on discernment and leadership at Woodbrooke Quaker Study Centre.

Bieber, N. (2011). *Decision Making & Spiritual Discernment: the sacred art of finding your way* (Paperback ed.). Skylight Paths.

Bill, B. (2008). *Sacred Compass – the Way of Spiritual Discernment*. Paraclete Press.

Coogan, U. (2016, Sept 20). A conversation on discernment and spiritual direction.

Cox, G. (2014). *A Quaker Approach to Research: Collaborative Practice and Communal Discernment*. Quaker Institute for the Future.

CTUCC (The Connecticut Conference United Church of Christ). (2014). *The Discernment Process. 10 Movements*. Retrieved Sept 10th, 2016, from http://www.ctucc.org/resources/discernmentprocess.html

Dawes, J., Dolley, J., & Isaksen, I. (2005). *The Quest, Exploring A Sense of Soul*. O Books.

Eccles, P. (2009). *The Presence in the Midst*. Quaker Books.

Experiment with Light Network. (2015). Retrieved Sept 3rd, 2016, from http://www.experiment-with-light.org.uk/about.htm

Experiment with Light Network, (2016). *Experiment with Light Journal*. Issue 20 2016, page 16. Retrieved October 23, 2016, from http://www.experiment-with-light.org.uk/ewlnl20.pdf

Farnham, S. G., Gill, J. P., McLean, R. T., & Ward, S. M. (2011). *Listening Hearts*. Morehouse Publishing.

Farnham, S. G., Hull, S. A., & McLean, R. T. (1996). *Grounded in God*. Morehouse Publishing.

Farrow, J. (1989). *Discernment in the Quaker Tradition*. The Way Supplement 64, 51-62.

Gwyn, D. (2014). *A Sustainable Life* (1st ed.). QuakerPress of Friends General Conference.

Hardy, A. (1979). *The Spiritual Nature of Man, a study of contemporary religious experience*. Oxford University Press.

Hay, D. (2006). *Something There, the biology of the human spirit* (Paperback ed.). Dartman Longman & Todd.

Heathfield, M. (1994). *Being Together: Our Corporate Life in the Religious Society of Friends*. Quaker Books.

Hewitson, G. (2013). *Journey Into Life*. 2013 Swarthmore Lecture. London: Quaker Books.

Hewitson, G. (2014, October). *Learning to Stand Fearlessly in Powerful Powerlessness*. Retrieved October 21st, 2016, from http://quakersinwales.org.uk/wp-content/uploads/powerful_powerlessness_gwtalkoct2014.pdf

Hutchinson, M. (2016, February 27th). Concerns and the role of local and area meetings in corporate discernment.

James, W. (1902). *The Varieties of Religious Experience, a study in human nature*. Longmans Green & Co.

Jaworski, J. (2012). *Source: the inner path of knowledge creation* (ebook).

Jaworski, J. (2014). *Bohm's Infinite Potential*. Retrieved Sept 28th, 2016, from http://www.josephjaworski.com/bohms-infinite-potential/#more-162

Jaworski, J. (2014). *When the Lines Begin to Cross, Profound Experience Leading to Discovery*. Retrieved Sept 28th, 2016, from http://www.josephjaworski.com/direct-experience-confirmed-lines-begin-cross/#more-137

Junker, L. (2005). *Friends' Practice of Group Spiritual Discernment*. Retrieved June 23rd, 2016, from http://www.quakerinfo.com/junker_discernment.pdf

Karban, R. (2015). *Plant Sensing and Communication*. (Reviewed) University of Chicago Press. Retrieved July 23rd, 2016, from http://ucanr.edu/blogs/blogcore/postdetail.cfm?postnum=18412

Khema, A. (2002). *Being Nobody, Going Nowhere*: Meditations on the Buddhist Path (Paperback ed.). Wisdom Publications.

Liebert, E. (2008). *The Way of Discernment – Spiritual Practices for Decision Making* (Paperback ed.). Westminster John Know Press.

Liebert, E. (2015). *The Soul of Discernment: a Spiritual Practice for Communities and Institutions*. Westminster John Knox Press.

Life and Leadership. (2012). *Review: Morris and Olsen, Discerning God's Will Together*. Retrieved August 25th, 2016, from http://www.lifeandleadership.com/book-summaries/morris-and-olsen-discerning-gods-will-together.html

Lonsdale, D. (1992). *Dance to the Music of the Spirit: The Art of Discernment*. Darton, Longman & Todd Ltd.

Loring, P. (1992). *Spiritual Discernment: the context and goal of clearness committees*. Pendle Hill Pamphlet 305. Pendle Hill Publications.

Loring, P. (1997). *Listening Spirituality Volume 1. Personal Spiritual Practices Among Friends*. Openings Press.

Loring, P. (1999). *Listening Spirituality Volume 2. Corporate Spiritual Practice Among Friends*. Openings Press.

Loring, P. (2016). *Quaker Speak: The Quaker Practice of Discernment*. Retrieved August 5th, 2016, from https://m.youtube.com/watch?v=PfIG2m7dAk8

Mace, J. (2012). *God and Decision-making*. Quaker Books.

Mancuso, S. & Viola, A. (2015). *Brilliant Green: the surprising history and science of plant intelligence* (review). Retrieved July 22nd, 2016, from New Scientist: www.newscientist.com/article/mg22630230-300-intelligent-life-why-dont-we-consider-plants-to-be-smart/

Martin, M. (2016). *Shifting to the Heart*. Retrieved Sept 2nd, 2016, from https://awholeheart.com/2016/03/29/shifting-to-the-heart/

McIntosh, A. (2008). *Engaging Walter Wink's Powers – an activist's testimony*. In Seiple and Weidmann (Eds.), Enigmas and Powers (pp. 101-112). Princeton Theological Monograph, Pickwick Publications.

Moran, J. (2016, Sept 13th). Personal correspondence.

Morris, D., & Olsen, C. (2012). *Discerning God's Will Together* (Revised and Updated. Pbk ed.). Alban Institute Inc.

Muers, R., & Grant, R. (2016). *Thinking Through Threshing: report.* Retrieved Sept 26th, 2016, from http://www.leeds.ac.uk/arts/downloads/125029/research/

Murray, W. H. (1951). *The Scottish Himalaya Expedition.*

NPC; New Philanthropy Capital. (2009). *Assessment of Quaker Social Action.* Retrieved Oct 4th, 2016, from http://www.thinknpc.org/publications/charity-analysis-quaker.../quaker-social-action/

Palmer, P. J. (2004). *A Hidden Wholeness – a Journey Toward an Undivided Life* (1st ed.). Jossey-Bass.

Palmer, P. J. (2009). *The Clearness Committee – a Communal Approach to Discernment.* Retrieved Sept 14th, 2016, from http://www.couragerenewal.org/PDFs/Parker-Palmer_Clearness-Committee.pdf

Pearn, J. (2017). *The language of leadings: a reflection on faith, action and concern* Forthcoming publication by Quaker Books

Presencing. (2016). Presencing Institute. Retrieved July 23, 2016, from https://www.presencing.com/presencing

Presencing Institute. (n.d.). *Summary Overview: Theory U - Leading from the Future As It Emerges.* Retrieved Sept 3rd, 2016, from https://www.presencing.com/sites/default/files/page-files/Theory_U_2pageOverview.pdf

Presencing Institute. (n.d.). Tools. Retrieved Sept 18th, 2016, from https://www.presencing.com/tools

Pullman, P. (1995). *Northern Lights* (UK (US *The Golden Compass*, Knopf) ed.). Scholastic.

Quaker Faith & Practice (QFP) ; Britain Yearly Meeting of the Religious Society of Friends. (2016). *Quaker Faith and Practice.* Retrieved July 21, 2016, from http://qfp.quaker.org.uk/

Quaker Life, (2011). *Threshing Meetings.* BYM (Britain Yearly Meeting of the Religious Society of Friends) .

Quaker Social Action. (2013). *The Q-bit, at the heart of a Quaker-led organisation.*

QuakerSpeak. (2016). *The Quaker Practice of Discernment.* (YouTube) Retrieved Sept 1st, 2016, from https://www.youtube.com/watch?v=PfIG2m7dAk8

QUNO Geneva. (2016). Personal papers.

Rogers, C. (1996). *A Way of Being.* Houghton Mifflin.

Rohr, R. (2015). *Richard Rohr on "The Cloud of Unknowing".* Retrieved Sept 19, 2016, from https://universalistfriends.org/weblog/richard-rohr-on-the-cloud-of-unknowing

Scharmer, O. &. Kaufer, K. (2013). *Leading from the Emerging Future: from ego-system to eco-system economies* (e-book ed.). Berrett-Koehler Publishers.

Scharmer, O. (2007). *Theory U: Executive Summary of Leading from the Future.* Retrieved July 23rd, 2016, from Presencing Institute Executive Summaries: https://www.presencing.com/sites/default/files/page-files/Theory_U_Exec_Summary.pdf

Scharmer, O. (2009). *Theory U Presentation – Presencing / Levels of Listening.* Retrieved Sept 3rd, 2016, from https://www.presencing.com/sites/default/files/tools/UPresentation_v2.1.ppt

Scharmer, O. (2009). *Theory U, Leading From the Future as it Emerges.* (Kindle). Berrett-Koehler.

Scharmer, O. (2015). *MiT ULab: Transforming business, society and self:* Source book.

Scharmer, O. (2015). *Otto Scharmer on the Four Levels of Listening.* Retrieved Sept 3rd, 2016, from https://www.youtube.com/watch?v=eLfXpRkVZaI

Scharmer, O. (n.d.). *Addressing the Blind Spot: Executive Summary from Theory U leading from the future as it emerges.* Retrieved Oct 3rd, 2016, from https://www.presencing.com/sites/default/files/page-files/Theory_U_2pageOverview.pdf

SE Scotland Area Quaker Meeting. (2016). Concerns and the role of local and area meetings in corporate discernment.

Senge, P. M. (2005). *Presence. Exploring profound change in people, organizations and society.* London: Nicholas Brealey Publishing.

Steere, D. (1971). *Mutual Irradiation: a Quaker View of Ecumenism*. Pendle Hill Pamphlet 175. Pendle Hill Publications.

Steere, D. (2005). *Quaker Spirituality: Selected Writings* (Reprint edition ed.). Spiritual Classics HarperOne.

Steere, D. (1955). *Where Words Come From* (1st ed.). George Allen & Unwin Ltd.

Stephenson, R. (2013). *Faith, Discernment and Trust*. The Friend, 171, No 47 (21 November), 6-7.

Sweeney, L. S. (2014). *Moving into a Deeper Communion: Communal Discernment through Contemplative Dialogue*. Retrieved August 25th, 2015, from http://www.srcharitycinti.org/members/chapter/Liz%20Sweeney,%20SSJ.pdf

Taber, W. (1992). *Four Doors to Meeting for Worship*. Pendle Hill Pamphlet 306. Philadelphia: Pendle Hill Publications.

Wilson, R. (2007). *Authority, Leadership and Concern*, Swarthmore Lecture 1949 (2nd ed.). Quaker Books.

Woolley, J. (2016, May 28). Personal discussion – use of Theory U by QUNO Geneva Central Committee